"Revelation is one of my favo[...]
Duvall is one of my favorite authors and commentators on
the Bible. That makes for a great combination in *The Heart
of Revelation*. This book is biblical theology for the church
at its best."

—**Daniel L. Akin**, president, Southeastern
Baptist Theological Seminary

"*The Heart of Revelation* illuminates this challenging and complex biblical book for contemporary readers by unraveling its
mysteries in a fresh and thematic manner. Scott Duvall is to
be heartily commended for providing this clear guide that will
enable students, teachers, and pastors to comprehend and communicate the riches so often missed in the Bible's concluding
book. It is truly a joy and a delight to welcome and recommend
this outstanding and insightful exploration of these ten central
and overarching themes in the book of Revelation."

—**David S. Dockery**, chancellor, Trinity
International University

"Many find the book of Revelation confusing or intimidating.
In *The Heart of Revelation*, Scott Duvall opens up one of the
most fascinating books of the Bible and explains it in a way
people can understand. Add this book to your library!"

—**Nick Floyd**, senior pastor,
Cross Church, Northwest Arkansas

"Scott Duvall's *The Heart of Revelation* offers the perfect blend
of sound biblical interpretation, rich theological reflection, and
practical application, complete with small-group discussion
questions at the end of each chapter. I love this book and cannot wait to use it in the church and with my students."

—**George H. Guthrie**, professor of New
Testament, Regent College

"Brilliantly practical. That is who Scott Duvall is, and what he has written in *The Heart of Revelation*. Without cutting corners or oversimplifying biblical texts he has hung the content of one of the most difficult books of the bible on ten hooks, making this book brilliantly practical and a must read for serious followers of Jesus."

—**Alex Himaya**, senior pastor, theChurchat, Tulsa, OK

"Studying the book of Revelation can often be overwhelming and even discouraging. With so many opinions and varying positions taken related to its content, we can lose sight of the big picture God is communicating. This is where *The Heart of Revelation* helps the most. Rather than bringing confusion to this subject, Duvall brings clarity to a complex book that is ultimately meant to provide encouragement and hope. As a local church pastor, I am always looking for resources that will help put topics like Revelation on a shelf everyone can reach and anyone can understand. Duvall has accomplished this. I encourage any student of the Bible desiring to grow in the understanding of Scripture to get their hands on this great book."

—**Jarrett Stephens**, teaching pastor,
Prestonwood Baptist Church, Plano, TX

"Scott Duvall has gleaned the essential themes of hope from the mysterious field of the Revelation of John. With a scholar's mind and a pastor's heart, he unpacks for the reader ten topics from the book that support its primary message: 'God Wins!' From the 'Cast of Characters' at the front of the book to the community group questions at the end of each chapter, Duvall leads the reader through the maze of symbols, images, and cryptic language to grasp God's promise of a new heaven and new earth where God sits on his eternal throne. If your group wants to study the Revelation, go through this study first. All the others will make sense after it."

—**C. Gene Wilkes**, president, B. H.
Carroll Theological Institute

THE HEART OF
REVELATION

REVISED EDITION

THE HEART OF
REVELATION

◆ ◆ ◆ ◆ ◆ ◆ ◆ ◆ ◆

UNDERSTANDING THE 10 ESSENTIAL
THEMES OF THE BIBLE'S FINAL BOOK

J. SCOTT DUVALL

ACADEMIC
NASHVILLE, TENNESSEE

The Heart of Revelation, Revised Edition
Copyright © 2019 by J. Scott Duvall

Published by B&H Academic
Nashville, Tennessee

All rights reserved.

ISBN: 978-1-5359-8199-6

Dewey Decimal Classification: 228

Subject Heading: BIBLE. N.T. REVELATION—STUDY AND
TEACHING / END OF THE WORLD / ESCHATOLOGY

To our beautiful and beloved daughters,
Ashley, Amy, and Meagan

May God give you the grace, wisdom, and courage to be
victorious and to "follow the Lamb wherever he goes"
(Rev 14:4).

CONTENTS

Contents

ACKNOWLEDGMENTS

The book of Revelation has been opened to me through the writings of Christian scholars. I'm deeply indebted to the contributions of Robert Mounce, Grant Osborne, Craig Keener, Greg Beale, Richard Bauckham, Colin Hemer, Eckhard Schnabel, and Mark Wilson. I'm especially grateful for Dr. Thomas "Tommy" D. Lea, former professor of New Testament at Southwestern Seminary. I was Dr. Lea's grader and a student in his Revelation class. My fascination with and love for the book of Revelation began in that classroom. May he rest in peace.

I'm thankful to the students who have taken my Revelation class over the past decade—for your insights, questions, and perceptive comments.

Thank you to my co-worker and friend Anna Sikes, who read the entire manuscript and provided extremely useful feedback on how others might hear what I was trying to say. Anna, may the Lord bless you as you continue your ministry at Ouachita.

To my wife, Judy, for your helpful feedback and ongoing support. God graced me beyond words when he gave me you as a life partner.

Most important, I'm grateful to God Almighty; to Jesus Christ, the Faithful Witness; and to the ever-present Holy Spirit. To you, the triune God, be all glory and praise!

INTRODUCTION

One Weird Book

Revelation is the strangest book in the whole Bible. In chapter 6, a Lamb opens six seals on a scroll that lead to riders on different-colored horses dealing out judgments. Then souls under the heavenly altar cry out to God, followed by a huge earthquake, causing the sun to turn black and the moon bloodred and the whole world to come apart. In the rest of the book, we read about the 144,000, the great multitude in heaven, locusts from the Abyss, John eating a little scroll, two witnesses, a red dragon and two beasts, Armageddon, Babylon the Great, a heavenly warrior on a white horse, the Millennium, the lake of fire, and the new Jerusalem coming out of the sky. The list of strange images is bewildering to say the least. If you're both drawn to Revelation and confused by it, you're not alone.

Two Popular Responses to Revelation

The strangeness of Revelation compared to the rest of the New Testament explains the two main ways people respond to it. Some people read it once and never want to read it again. It's just too weird. They are content to leave Revelation alone.

THE HEART OF REVELATION

A second common response to Revelation is to obsess over it. These people have read it dozens, perhaps even hundreds, of times. They have also read all the novels and watched all the movies and listened to all the preachers that deal with Revelation. They are into all things apocalyptic, convinced that we are living in the last days, where all the predictions of Revelation are coming true.

A Promising Third Way

It certainly seems as if all of Christendom responds to Revelation in one of these two ways: willful ignorance or fanatical obsession. I think both responses are wrong. I'm convinced there is a third way of reading the book in context that allows us to understand and live out its main message. If we ignore the book, we miss out on the concluding chapter to the entire story of the Bible, a chapter full of hope and encouragement. Who wants to read a whole book and not finish the last chapter? The church today desperately needs the vision of hope that Revelation provides. On the other hand, great harm comes to the church when we try to make Revelation all about us—how we must avoid the mark of the beast, or when the rapture will occur, or how we can identify the Antichrist. We have to read Revelation in context, or we will distort its message.

What to Expect from *The Heart of Revelation*

In this book, I will follow this promising third way of reading and applying Revelation by looking at the big picture and answering the question, What are the main truths and realities of Revelation that we can know for certain? I've identified the following ten themes as the most important ones in Revelation: God, worship, the people of God, the Holy Spirit, our enemies, the mission, Jesus Christ, judgment, the new creation, and perseverance. We will move back and forth within the book of Revelation as we study these ten themes. As you read through this book, it will help you to also read through the book of Revelation. At the end of each chapter I have included a reading plan that will take you through the entire book in the order of the biblical themes and a list of key texts for each theme. My hope is that as you learn what Revelation teaches on each theme, you will grasp the main message of this dramatic final chapter of the Bible and its relevance for the Christian life.

This isn't a technical, scholarly book, but I've also tried to write in light of the most reliable evangelical scholarship. The chapters are short, and each one has discussion questions for small groups. If you happen to lead such a small group, or if you want to dig even deeper into Revelation, please check out my commentary on Revelation in the Teach the Text Commentary Series (Grand Rapids: Baker Books, 2014). I wrote *The Heart of Revelation* for serious Christians who want to know the main teachings of Revelation. I hope you enjoy it, and I pray that it will strengthen your walk with the Lord Jesus Christ and bring you hope, courage, and wisdom.

Taking the Context Seriously

We must take the context of God's Word seriously if we claim to take its message seriously.[1] To hear what God is saying to us in Revelation, we must first hear what God said to the first Christians who heard its amazing message.[2] Who were those people, and what was their situation?

The Seven Churches and Their Situation

Revelation was written to Christians living in Asia Minor in the first century, either during the reign of Roman Emperor Domitian (AD 95–96) or around AD 69, shortly after Emperor Nero's death in 68 and before the fall of Jerusalem in 70.

The book begins "The revelation from [or "of," CSB] Jesus Christ, which God gave him to show his servants what must soon take place. He made it known by sending his angel to his servant John, who testifies to everything he saw—that is, the word of God and the testimony of Jesus Christ" (1:1–2). The revelation is "of/from Jesus Christ," meaning that it is a book about Jesus (the central figure) but also a book from Jesus. The revelation moves through a chain of communication from God through Jesus to his servants. One of these servants is John, the author of Revelation (1:1, 4, 9–10; 22:8–9). John is the one who received and recorded the heavenly visions for the churches of Asia while suffering exile on the island of Patmos for carrying out his prophetic witness to Christ. As a result, the message of Revelation is from Jesus (and sometimes Jesus speaks directly, such as in 1:17–3:22), but it's written by John, both the recipient of the visions and the author of the book. Revelation, then, is both a spiritual vision given to a prophet and a literary masterpiece inspired by God. Historically, most church leaders have identified this "John" as the apostle John, who wrote the Gospel of John.

John wrote to seven particular churches in Asia Minor (modern-day Turkey). What was life like for the Christians in the seven churches? Short answer: life was hard. In the Roman Empire everything pointed to the idea that Caesar is Lord! Since the basic Christian confession is "Jesus is Lord," there was an inherent conflict between those who believed Caesar was Lord and those who followed Jesus as Lord.

Christians faced pressure from three sources. First, they were pressured by Rome itself. Rome was persecuting Christians, but that wasn't happening in every little village across the empire. In general, the pressure from Rome was subtler and more seductive. Rome opposed the church mainly through what is known as the *imperial cult*, a system of influences (political, social, economic, military, religious) that promoted the worship of the emperor. (The term "cult" in biblical scholarship often refers to a system of worship and devotion.) There were temples, priests, festivals,

coins, statues, trade guilds, and other symbols of empire that pointed to Caesar as Lord. But to worship the emperor directly contradicted the most basic Christian confession: "Jesus is Lord" (cf. 2:13; 17:6; 18:24; 19:2). When Christians refused to participate in pagan temple worship and festivals connected with emperor worship, they experienced negative social, political, and economic consequences. Because many of the imperial cult activities promoted idolatrous and immoral behavior, Christians refused to join in. As a result, they were viewed as anti-Rome and faced rejection and even persecution.

Second, Christians were pressured by the Jews. Judaism was respected within the Roman Empire as an ancient monotheistic religion, and Jews were exempted from worshiping Roman gods and participating in the imperial cult. Some Jews were hostile toward the church and brought charges against Christians before the Roman authorities, accusing them of being anti-Roman troublemakers. This very thing apparently happened in Smyrna; Jesus reassures the believers of Smyrna with these words: "I know about the slander of those who say they are Jews and are not, but are a synagogue of Satan" (2:9). Likewise, we also see pressure from Jews in Philadelphia; to the believers there, Jesus promises justice: "I will make those who are of the synagogue of Satan, who claim to be Jews though they are not, but are liars—I will make them come and fall down at your feet and acknowledge that I have loved you" (3:9).

Third, Christians were pressured by false teachers connected to the seven churches. Within some of these congregations were influential members who urged believers to go along with the surrounding culture to avoid hardship, especially economic hardship. Teachers such as Jezebel and her followers (2:20–24) and the Nicolaitans (2:6, 14–15) tempted believers to be disloyal to Christ and his ways in order to conform to the world.

There were basically two responses to this pressure to conform to the world. Some were standing strong against the idolatry and immorality promoted by an ungodly empire and were, as a result, facing persecution. Others were caving in to the pressure of the empire and compromising their faith.

The Purpose of Revelation: Who Is Lord?

Revelation comforts and assures the faithful who are suffering but sternly warns those who are compromising with the world system. This double message of comfort and warning is central to the overall purpose of the book. Revelation uses powerful visions and symbols to overpower the symbols of a wicked empire, whether that is Rome or any future ungodly empire. Revelation answers the basic question, Who is Lord of the universe: Jesus Christ or Caesar?

Since Christians lived within the Roman Empire, they were reminded daily of Rome's power as they passed by temples dedicated to an emperor or used coins with Caesar's face on them or saw statues of the emperor, and so on. (We may use coins with a president's face on them, but we don't see temples honoring that president as a god, and we're not pressured to worship him as such.) All of the symbols they encountered cried out, "Caesar is Lord, and you should worship him." Christians desperately needed to see reality from God's perspective.

When you hear or read Revelation, it's like putting on a VR headset in order to see true spiritual reality. In Revelation, God defeats the powers of darkness, judges evil, rescues his people, and transforms creation. The book unveils or reveals reality from God's perspective. As a result, the Caesar images of this world are replaced with heavenly images of God's sovereign rule over the universe. By transforming your mind and imagination, Revelation empowers you to reenter your present world and live faithfully. If I had to sum up the whole message of Revelation in two words, I would say, "God wins!"

In the end, Revelation is about hope. No matter how difficult and desperate life appears now, Revelation reminds us that one day Jesus will return to defeat his enemies, rescue his people, and restore his creation. One day God will judge evil and live among his people in a new heaven and new earth. To persevere faithfully, to remain steadfast, to hang in there over the long haul, we must have hope. Revelation gives us a sure and certain hope in a world that is sometimes hostile toward us. God's victory is certain!

How Does Revelation Communicate?

Revelation combines three types of literature to communicate its message. First, it's a *letter*. As such, Revelation targets a specific audience: the seven churches in the province of Asia (1:11). These seven locations are named in the order in which a letter carrier might visit them, starting from Patmos (the place of John's exile) and moving in a clockwise direction. New Testament letters were meant to be read aloud to believers gathered for worship (1:3; 22:18–19) and were written to address a particular situation or problem. While the message of Revelation certainly extends beyond these seven churches, any responsible approach to interpreting the book must start with its message to the seven churches.

Revelation also claims to be a *prophecy* (1:3; 22:7, 10, 18–19; cf. 19:10; 22:9), which includes the idea of predicting the future and proclaiming God's truth in the present. Surprisingly, most of the time biblical prophecy is more about proclaiming than predicting, and the same holds true for Revelation. In the places where Revelation is described as a prophecy, readers are commanded to "take to heart" or obey the prophecy (1:3; 22:7, 18–19). How can you obey a prediction? You really can't. But you can obey a proclamation. Revelation speaks about the future, to be sure, but it speaks most forcefully about how God wants us to live in the present.

Finally, Revelation is an *apocalypse* (1:1; Gk. *apokalypsis*), a term meaning "unveiling" or "revelation." Apocalyptic literature focuses on God's communication to a well-known person (like John or Daniel) through visions with the message that God will intervene in the course of history to overthrow evil empires and establish his kingdom. We are told in 1:1 that God has "made it known" (NIV, ESV), a term that suggests God has communicated by means of signs or symbols. Also, we are told that God gave the revelation to Jesus to "show" to his servants (1:1; 4:1; 17:1; 21:9, 10; 22:1, 6), that is, to show through visions. In Revelation, God communicates through picture language to give hope to people living in a crisis situation. For instance, Revelation often portrays Jesus as the "Lamb of God." But you should not conclude that Jesus is a literal animal. The expression "Lamb of God" is a picture or symbol of Jesus's sacrificial death on the cross to take away our sins.

How Should We Interpret Revelation?

Before we go on to explore the ten most important themes of Revelation, I need to explain a bit more about how we can read Revelation responsibly.[3] I would like to suggest a few helpful guidelines for interpreting the book of Revelation:

1. We should try to discover the message to the original read-ers. You will be tempted to ignore the biblical audience and jump directly to what God is saying to us today. But remember, God originally spoke to the Christians in the seven churches of Asia Minor, and his message to us will be an extension of his message to them. If our interpre-tation makes no sense for the original readers, we have probably missed the real meaning of the passage.

2. We must take Revelation seriously, but we shouldn't always take it literally. Revelation conveys historical truth (Jesus died for our sins), but it uses picture language to do so (Jesus is the Lamb of God). The woman who sits on seven hills isn't an extremely large woman but a sym-bol for the city of Rome, a city built on seven hills. The new Jerusalem is in the shape of a cube, not because we will all be riding elevators for eternity, but because God's presence indwells the entire city (the holy of holies in the ancient temple, the place where God's presence dwelled, was cube shaped). Picture language can convey literal,

historical truth, but we should not always take it literally, or we will distort its message. Instead, we should look for what the image or symbol represents. To understand the images, we must look to what John himself says, to the historical context, and to the Old Testament. When John identifies an image, we should pay close attention to what he says (e.g., in 1:13 the Son of Man is Christ; in 1:20 the golden lampstands are the churches; in 5:5–6 the Lion is the Lamb; in 12:9 the red dragon is Satan; and in 21:9–10 the new Jerusalem is the wife of the Lamb, or the church). Again, we should also study the historical context of the seven churches and turn to the Old Testament to discover the meaning of the images.

3. We should focus on the main theological message of each vision. It's a mistake to think you have to understand 100 percent of Revelation or you can't understand any of it. While the details of this awesome and mysterious book are often debated, the central idea and the main points are clear: God is in control, and he will successfully accomplish his purposes.

As you read a section of Revelation, ask yourself, "What is the big idea of this section?" As you learn more about Revelation, you can come to a decision about the particulars. Just don't miss the big picture because you feel as if you have to know all the details now. When we come to a confusing section in class, I'll often ask my students, "Are these good guys or bad guys?" It's my way of zooming out to catch the big idea even when they don't at first understand the specifics.

Revelation is much more than an end-times puzzle to be solved; rather, it is God's communication to the seven churches (and by extension to the church in every age) about how to live faithfully in light of the future he has in store. You can still see the forest even when you can't identify all the trees.

I wrote *The Heart of Revelation* to help you understand the big picture of Revelation. I've come to love the book of Revelation because it speaks powerfully and deeply about every aspect of the Christian life. It brings tremendous hope that the great story we are living does, in fact, have a happy ending. God wins, and we do too! As you read this book and learn more about its ten most important themes, I pray that you will find yourself knowing and loving God even more than you do now. And I pray that your hope will become even more sure and certain, even as we live in increasingly uncertain times. Most of all, I pray for you the admonition that Jesus gave to each of the seven churches: "Whoever has ears, let them hear what the Spirit says to the churches" (e.g., 2:7).

CAST OF CHARACTERS IN THE DIVINE DRAMA OF REVELATION[1]

Abyss A term used seven times in Revelation to refer to the abode/prison for the demonic locusts and their king, Apollyon, the beast, and Satan himself during the Millennium (9:1, 2, 11; 11:7; 17:8; 20:1, 3).

Armageddon The epic eschatological battle between God and the forces of evil (16:12–16). This battle is anticlimactic since Christ conquers merely by his appearance and his word of judgment.

Babylon the Great The term "Babylon" is used six times in Revelation to symbolize any great center of pagan power (14:8; 16:19; 17:5; 18:2, 10, 21). The early Christians referred to Rome as Babylon (1 Pet 5:13).

Balaam Those who hold to the teachings of Balaam are a group of false teachers who encouraged Christians to use their freedom to participate in pagan worship activities, including the worship of the Roman emperor (Rev 2:14).

beast from the earth A figure representing pagan religious power in service of the wicked political/military/economic

13

power structures and their evil leaders (13:11–12). This figure is also called the "false prophet" in Revelation (16:13; 19:20; 20:10), pointing to its religious role in promoting the worship of the first beast (e.g., the priesthood of the imperial cult, a religious system promoting the worship of the emperor and other pagan deities).

beast from the sea A figure representing political, military, and economic power used in the service of Satan (13:1–2). Often such pagan power is personified in a single wicked leader (e.g., Nero or Domitian in first-century Rome and Hitler in Nazi Germany). The final eschatological leader has traditionally been identified with this beast and called the Antichrist, although that term is never used in Revelation.

book of life / Lamb's book of life The register of all true believers, those who have been granted heavenly citizenship (3:5).

bride/wife of the Lamb A symbol for God's holy people, the church (19:7–8). The marriage metaphor reveals the depth and fullness of God's covenant love for his people and his plan to live forever with them in the new creation.

death and Hades The term "Hades" refers to the realm of the dead (1:18; 6:8; 20:13, 14), not to the place of final punishment, or "hell" (cf. 20:14–15). Death is the last enemy and, along with Hades, will one day be thrown into the lake of fire, symbolizing the final and total destruction of death.

every tribe, language, people, and nation Variations of this expression occur seven times in Revelation to indicate universality (5:9; 7:9; 10:11; 11:9; 13:7; 14:6; 17:15). When referring to the faithful, it emphasizes the multicultural people of God (5:9).

fiery lake of burning sulfur Whereas "Hades" refers to the grave or realm of the dead, the lake of fire is equivalent to Gehenna, or what is traditionally understood as "hell." This place of final punishment is the second (or eternal) death (20:14–15) for all of God's enemies.

four living creatures An exalted order of angels resembling the cherubim of Ezekiel 1 and 10 as well as the seraphim of Isaiah 6. They represent God's creation, stand closest to God's presence, play some role in executing judgment, and lead the heavenly court in worship (Rev 4:6–8).

great city (Sodom, Egypt, Jerusalem) A symbol for any center of worldly power allied against God and his people (11:7–8). Rome was likely in view in the first century. This wicked city is a place of moral depravity, of oppression, and of opposition to Christ.

great multitude The church triumphant that has come through the great tribulation and now celebrates God's victory in heaven (7:9). This multicultural people of God is the heavenly counterpart to the 144,000 engaged in battle on earth.

great prostitute / woman sitting on the beast A great center of pagan power (i.e., Babylon), undoubtedly referring to Rome in the first century (17:1–18; 19:2). She leads others to join her in idolatry and immorality and stands in contrast to the bride of Christ depicted in Revelation 19–22.

great supper of God The final judgment of the wicked, where the birds of prey consume the dead bodies of God's enemies (19:17–18). This eschatological feast stands in contrast to the wedding supper of the Lamb for the righteous. Here the wicked actually become the feast, or the supper.

great white throne The site of final judgment, when those who have not been given resurrection bodies (i.e., all unbelievers) will stand before God to face eternal punishment (20:11–15).

holy city / new Jerusalem The new creation (new heaven and new earth), where God will live forever among his people (21:9–21). The old Jerusalem with its temple gives way to the heavenly city, where the entire city will be a temple or dwelling place of God.

inhabitants of the earth An expression that is used consistently to depict unbelievers who rebel against God and suffer his judgment (3:10).

Jezebel A prophetess in Thyatira who promoted idolatry and immorality, likely by teaching that Christians could join the trade guilds and participate in the pagan worship feasts without compromising their faith (2:20). Throughout the history of God's people, Jezebel has become an enduring symbol of idolatry and wickedness.

a kingdom and priests A description of the church, which fulfills the promise first made to Israel in Exod 19:5–6. God's people are kingdom citizens who will reign with Christ, as well as priests with all the privileges and responsibilities of serving him (Rev 5:10).

kings from the East / kings of the whole world Most often pagan political powers who commit adultery with the great prostitute and are allied with the beast (16:12–16). The likely background is Ezekiel 38–39, where Gog and Magog depict human enemies who war against God's people. As a contrast, Rev 21:24 highlights redeemed nations and kings.

Lamb An image that combines the background of the Passover lamb of Exodus 11–12 with the Suffering Servant lamb of Isaiah 52–53 to represent Jesus Christ (Rev 5:6).

mark of the beast A phrase used seven times in Revelation to symbolize ownership, identification, and allegiance (13:16, 17; 14:9, 11; 16:2; 19:20; 20:4). This image provides a figurative portrayal of a person's commitments and loyalties reflected in his or her ethical choices and objects of worship. This mark is deliberately received by unbelievers and stands in direct contrast to the seal of the living God given to believers.

nations The people of the world, who either follow Satan or follow God. The term is used both negatively (e.g., 14:8; 17:15; 18:23; 20:8) and positively (e.g., 5:9; 7:9; 21:24, 26; 22:2) in Revelation. Some among the nations oppose God and his people

16

(equivalent in this sense to "inhabitants of the earth"), while others respond in faith. Christ has redeemed some from among the nations, but only those who follow Christ will become citizens of the new Jerusalem.

new heaven and new earth The expression depicting the eternal state of the new creation, where God will live forever among his people (21:1–8). This completely transformed physical universe is also described as the holy city (or new Jerusalem), a temple city, and a garden city.

new song A celebration by God's people of the mighty and marvelous things God has done in conquering his enemies and providing salvation in Christ (5:9). Only the redeemed are allowed to sing this new song, implying that they have endured as faithful followers of Jesus. Those who overcome will enjoy the victory celebration.

Nicolaitans A group of false teachers closely connected to the cults of Balaam (2:14) and Jezebel (2:20–23). They are attempting to redefine the faith to allow Christians to fit in with (and perhaps profit from) the surrounding culture, with its idolatry, immorality, deceit, and false worship (2:6, 15).

144,000 A number that results from taking twelve (the number symbolizing completeness as well as the people of God), squaring it, and then multiplying the result by 1,000 (signifying a very large, complete number). The resulting number represents all followers of Jesus or the true Israel of God now sealed and engaged in spiritual battle (7:4).

red dragon Also called the ancient serpent, the accuser, the devil, or Satan (12:3, 9–10, 12; 20:2). The red color alludes to his character of violence and 150hed, and the dragon image draws on the Old Testament idea that serpents and sea monsters represent evil forces generally. Satan is God's archenemy, the accuser and tempter of God's people, and the deceiver of the world. He was defeated decisively at the cross and resurrection of Christ, and his future destruction is certain.

scroll / little scroll The "scroll" (chap. 5) and the "little scroll" (chap. 10) probably both refer to God's plan for judging evil, redeeming his people, and transforming creation, a plan anchored in the death and resurrection of Christ and consummated at his return.

seal of the living God In contrast to the mark of the beast, this stamp is given only to Christ's followers and indicates God's ownership and spiritual protection of his people (7:1–8). The seal exempts believers not from persecution or suffering but from demonic defeat and the wrath of God. John may have in mind the Holy Spirit as the seal (cf. 2 Cor 1:22; Eph 1:13).

seven golden lampstands The seven churches of Asia Minor, and the first intended recipients of the transforming vision that is the book of Revelation (1:12–16, 20; cf. Zech 4:2–10).

seven spirits of God The sevenfold Holy Spirit (Rev 1:4; 3:1). The background is Zech 4:2–10, in which God's work is accomplished by his Spirit.

seven stars The angels of the seven churches (Rev 1:20). Throughout Revelation the term "angel" refers to a heavenly being. These angels could serve as guardian angels or as personifications of the prevailing spirit or character of each church. They identify with and serve the churches and represent them before God.

666 The number of the beast's name (13:17–18). Most appeal to the Jewish practice of gematria (the ancient practice, adopted by the Jews, of interpreting the meaning of words based on the numerical value of each letter) to calculate the numerical value of the name of a Roman emperor (likely "Nero Caesar"). To identify the beast as Nero does not exclude the possibility of future beasts and a final eschatological beast. The number could also symbolize how the beast falls short of the trinity of perfection (777) or the "number" of Jesus (888). Both emphasize that the beast is a complete failure.

throne A symbol of God's absolute sovereignty and majesty (4:2). God's throne or sovereign rule is the central image in the book, around which everything else revolves.

tree of life A symbol of eternal life in the presence of God, full of never-ending provision (22:1–5).

twenty-four elders An exalted order of angels that serves as part of the heavenly council and in some sense represents the people of God (twelve tribes and twelve apostles). Their primary role is related to worship, since they are often portrayed as falling down (4:4).

two witnesses / two olive trees / two lampstands Drawing on the background of Zechariah 4, these images represent the witnessing church and its role in reflecting God's presence in a hostile world (Rev 11:3–4). The number two probably comes from the need for two witnesses to constitute a valid legal testimony and the connection with the two olive trees (kingship and priesthood).

wedding supper of the Lamb The future fellowship/celebration of God with his people in the new creation (19:6–10). As the divine husband, God has promised his bride a lavish banquet celebrating his defeat of their enemies and his abundant provision. Overall, the image of a wedding supper conveys the personal, intimate, joyous time of fellowship that God is preparing for his people.

woman clothed with the sun A symbol representing the community of faith that gives birth to the Messiah—the faithful remnant within Israel (12:1–2). The woman cannot be the virgin Mary because of the reference in 12:17 to the "rest of her [the woman's] offspring."

1

GOD

"The Almighty"

Everyone I know wants their life to work. I've never met a person who has set out to be a miserable failure. A failed life starts when a person believes the lie that it's all about him. George MacDonald—a Scottish minister, English professor, and author who had a tremendous influence over C. S. Lewis, J. R. R. Tolkien, G. K. Chesterton, and others—once said that "the one principle of hell is—I am my own!"[1] Revelation says we are not our own and it's not all about us. We are not the center of the universe, and when we try to put ourselves (or anything else) in that place, life inevitably falls apart. You can prolong the crash with more money or power, but it will happen eventually.

Revelation tells us loudly and clearly that God is the true center! He alone can bear the weight of the world. He alone can bear the weight of your world, of your life. He alone can give us meaning and purpose and significance. Isn't it unbelievably stressful to try to be our own center or to try to make someone or something into that center? I'm not only talking about bad stuff, but I'm also referring to good things or people, such as a spouse or a ministry or a job or a hobby. There is no center other than God that can bear the heavy weight of our trust and hold our lives together.

Revelation is the most God-centered book in the whole Bible. It reminds us that God is the only true center when it shows us that God is in control, that he is more powerful than all competing gods, that he loves and cares about us, that he has a plan to fix this broken world, and that in the end he will rid the universe of every trace of evil. Revelation presents God as *the* Almighty, the only true center we can count on.

God Is in Control!

From the very start, John reassures us that God is in control: "John, To the seven churches in the province of Asia: Grace and peace to you from him who is, and who was, and who is to come. . . . 'I am the Alpha and the Omega,' says the Lord God, 'who is, and who was, and who is to come, the Almighty'" (1:4, 8). God is the one "who is, and who was, and who is to come," an expression that reflects God's description of himself to Moses as "I AM WHO I AM" (Exod 3:14). In that famous burning-bush conversation, God was basically telling Moses that he is the eternally self-existent. In other words, God has always been God, he is God, and he always will be God. Just as he has been in control of the past, so he will be in control of what is happening now and what will happen in the future. Even when it doesn't seem like it, he is eternally sovereign (Rev 4:9–11; 10:6; 15:7). We serve a God who is in control!

What is fascinating about the "was, and is, and is to come" statement is that the "is to come" part has dropped off in the last two places it is mentioned in Revelation (11:17; 16:5; cf. 1:4, 8; 4:8). In those places in Revelation, the future has already arrived. When we come into God's presence one day, the "is to come" will become our "is." The future will become the present for us, which reminds me of the section of Handel's "Hallelujah" chorus drawn from 11:15: "The kingdom of the world has become the kingdom of our Lord and of his Messiah, and he will reign for ever and ever."

Perhaps surprisingly, God speaks directly in Revelation only twice—1:8 and 21:5–6—and in both places he identifies himself as "the Alpha and the Omega" (the first and last letters of the Greek alphabet). It's synonymous with "the Beginning and the End" (21:6; 22:13), or "the First and the Last" (1:17; 22:13). Revelation is telling us that God bookends all of human history. He is both the starting line and the finish line, and the whole race in between. The one who controls both ends of history also stands sovereign over everything in the middle. Again, God is in control.

Revelation affirms God's sovereignty in subtle ways through the use of the term "was given" (Gk. *edothē*). This is known as a theological or divine passive and occurs throughout the book to highlight God's control of events. When the text says that something "was given" but doesn't mention who gave it, often God is the implied subject. God is doing the giving. For example, those carrying out God's judgments are "given" the judgments, and while God is not mentioned directly, he stands behind those judgments (e.g., 6:2; 9:1). Evil powers like the two beasts are "given" permission to act so that God stands sovereign even over the forces of evil (e.g., 13:7, 14). And God also stands behind the protection of his people (e.g., the woman "was given" the wings of an eagle in 12:14).

It's comforting to say, "God is in control," but what does this really mean? We can easily misunderstand this expression. Revelation isn't saying that God causes everything that happens. People sin in Revelation (read about the sins of the seven churches in chaps. 2–3), but God doesn't cause sin. In Revelation, God's people suffer, even die, but God doesn't delight in the murdering of his own people. God's being in control doesn't mean that he is the source of sin and evil.

God's sovereign control means that while Satan and sin and death may win some battles, God wins the war.

The Almighty King

On April 18, 2007, in the eastern Turkish city of Malatya, three Christians were brutally tortured and murdered: Necati Aydin, Uğur Yüksel, and Tilmann Geske. Revelation scholar Mark Wilson, who lives in Turkey and knew these men, writes:

> Before this, my understanding of martyrdom had been an academic one. I had read about [the early Christian martyrs] Ignatius . . . and Polycarp. . . . I had shared the story of their deaths with many visitors who came to Izmir. But suddenly the suffering of these early Christians was no longer abstract; we were part of the community that was mourning the tragic loss of brothers in Christ.[2]

Christians living in the West don't experience much persecution, and many of us are ignorant of the sufferings of our fellow believers around the world.[3] Thankfully, through books like Eric Metaxas's *Bonhoeffer* and Paul Marshall, Lela Gilbert, and Nina Shea's *Persecuted*, and organizations such as Open Doors and the Voice of the Martyrs, we are learning more about how Christians are suffering today worldwide.[4]

The Christians who first read (or heard) Revelation were much more familiar with persecution. Some were experiencing persecution, even death, for remaining faithful to Christ, but most were actually compromising with the prevailing culture. In the Roman Empire, Rome considered itself the center of the universe, and the emperor claimed to be Lord of all.

The original readers would have been deeply encouraged to hear John's favorite title for God: the "Almighty." In Greek, the Roman emperor was called by a similar name: *autokratōr*, or "one who rules by himself." No one on earth could compare to an emperor like Nero or Domitian. Temples and statues and coins constantly reminded the people of the emperor's enormous reach and power.

But Revelation uses an even more powerful title for God: the "Almighty" (Gk. *pantokratōr*), a term meaning "ruler over all" (the term *pan* is the Greek word for "all," and *kratōr* means "mighty").[5] What is a measly earthly empire to God, who is in charge of the whole universe? Revelation is telling us that God is more powerful than all competing rulers—all of them, everywhere. There is no emperor or king or president who can compare to the one who rules the world. Our God is indeed "King of the nations" (15:3).

Revelation doesn't just tell us that God is in charge; it shows us. Of all the book's symbols, there is one that pulls together all the others: the throne of God. John is getting a personalized angelic tour of the cosmos by receiving a series of visions. In his first vision (chaps. 2–3), he is shown the circumstances of the churches on earth, where some are remaining faithful and others are compromising. It's natural to ask, "If Christians within the Roman Empire are struggling to stay faithful, has God lost control?" or "If the goddess Roma (symbolizing Rome and her empire) can murder and seduce God's people, is God still in charge?" The throne image helps answer these kinds of questions.

After hearing about the situation of the seven churches, John is shown a vision of heaven so that he can see what's really real (4:1–11; cf. Isa 6:1–5). He's blown away by what he sees. He immediately lays eyes on the center of all reality: the majestic, glorious throne. God and the Lamb occupy the throne, and the Spirit of God blazes in brilliant light in front of the throne. Multitudes of angels surround the throne in concentric circles of never-ending worship. Kingdoms come and go, but God on his throne remains forever. The center of all reality is the triune God on his throne.

To say that God is seated on his throne doesn't mean that God is literally sitting in heaven in a giant chair, any more than saying Jesus is the Lamb of God means he is a four-legged animal. Rather, Revelation shows us through picture language that God is King over all competing kings and that he is the Ruler over all rival rulers. The throne image centers and anchors and grounds everything else. All of creation revolves around the throne, as the rim and spokes rotate around the hub of a bicycle wheel. All the subsequent visions in the book originate from the throne of God, the ultimate and true center of reality.

You probably recall that the first part of the Lord's Prayer from Matthew 6 is all about God—may we recognize your name as holy; may your kingdom come and your will be done, on earth as it is in heaven. Well, Revelation 4 shows us the "as in heaven" part of that prayer as we see worship happening now. What is happening in heaven now will one day spill over onto the new earth as God's will becomes the universal norm of the new creation.[6] What a day that will be!

The throne-room vision of Revelation 4 also helps us adopt a kingdom perspective for our lives now. We need a heavenly view of things to stay faithful in this world. While it appears that the powers of this world—whether they be political, religious, military, or economic—are having their way now, this is not the whole (or even the real) picture. These pretend gods are on a very short leash. Their kingdoms will not last. One day their royal charade will come crashing down as the kingdom of this world becomes the kingdom of our God.

Our Faithful Father

In Revelation, God is not just sitting on his throne, ruling the universe. God is high and lifted up for sure. He is transcendent, but he is not distant. He is closer to us than we are to ourselves.[7] He is also our faithful Father, who loves and cares for us, his beloved children.

I don't know all the reasons why, but it's been a struggle for me to believe that God really loves me. Some of you might have the same struggle. As it turns out, this is nothing new. From the very beginning, the evil one has been trying to convince us that God is withholding something from us, that he doesn't really want what is best for us. Adam and Eve fell for this lie back in Genesis 3. If we come to believe that God is less loving and less gracious than he truly is, we will turn elsewhere to get our needs met. When we decide that God doesn't have our best interest at heart, that he isn't really good (for us), then our picture of God becomes distorted, and we will struggle to trust him to give us life.

Revelation sends the clear message that God is for us, that he loves us, and that he will protect us from spiritual harm and bring us safely into his eternal kingdom. Do we get God's love like the apostle John got it? If the same John wrote both Revelation and the Gospel of John (as many evangelical scholars believe), then how cool is it to remember that he refers to himself as "the disciple whom Jesus loved" (John 13:23; cf. 20:2; 21:7, 20)? This doesn't mean that he saw himself as Jesus's favorite or that he felt more loved than the other apostles. He just got it. What shaped his identity and self-understanding more than anything else was Jesus's great love for him.

We can, of course, go too far and conclude that God is *only* loving and gracious, not holy or righteous or truthful. But that kind of God wouldn't really be loving at all, would he? Someone who doesn't want what is right or who doesn't tell us the truth doesn't really love us. But most of the time, our struggle runs in the other direction: to believe deep down that God really does love us and that he will always be faithful to us and do us good.

In Revelation, God is portrayed as the Father of our Lord Jesus Christ and, by implication, our Father also. Jesus promises to acknowledge the names of those who overcome before his Father (3:5) and that these victors will be enthroned with him just as he has been enthroned with the Father (3:21). In chapter 14, we read about these same victors standing with the Lamb on Mount Zion. They are portrayed as those who have the Lamb's name and his Father's name written on their foreheads, a sign that his people belong to him in a secure and permanent relationship (14:1).

The reality of God's fatherly love for us appears most personally in Revelation 21. When the new creation is revealed, a heavenly voice announces that God's dwelling place is now among the people. They will be his people, and he will be their God. Then we read that God will "wipe every tear from their eyes" (21:4) and "they will be my children" (21:7). You may have received love from your parents, or they may have withheld love from you. But one thing you can count on: your heavenly Father loves you perfectly. If you are a follower of Jesus Christ, you are the Father's child. And one day he will embrace you and wipe away your tears of suffering with his gentle hand.

Revelation reminds us that God loves and cares for us in many other ways (e.g., how he answers our prayers—see 5:8; 8:3–4), but one way deserves special attention. While God pours out his judgments on the wicked, he shelters and protects his people from his wrath. The "seal of the living God" (7:2–5; 9:4) stands in contrast to the "mark of the beast" (16:2; 19:20). Christians have received the seal of the living God, so they need not fear receiving the mark of the beast. Everyone has one of these two marks, never both. Those who are not sealed by God will be deceived by evil forces and suffer God's wrath (13:7–8; 14:9–11). Although God's seal doesn't exempt us from persecution and physical suffering, it does protect us from spiritual harm and free us from his coming judgment. The apostle Paul equates God's seal with the Holy Spirit (see 2 Cor 1:22; Eph 1:13; 4:30), and this is probably what John has in mind as well. How comforting it is to know that we are sealed and protected and guarded by God! Nothing can separate us from God's love (read Rom 8:1, 31–39 to get the picture in other words).[8]

Our view of God has enormous implications for our spiritual health. Lies about God will stunt our growth and hold us back, while a true view of God will liberate us and cause our relationship to grow and flourish. We need to take to heart what Revelation tells us about God. Sometimes it's good to repeat the truths that you see in Scripture as a way of driving them down deep: God loves me. God cares deeply for me. God shelters and protects me. God hears my prayers. God is always faithful.

Alan Scholes speaks of having two views of God: a mental view (what we say we believe about God) and an emotional view (how we truly feel about him).[9] To correct a deficient mental view of God, we need to study the Scriptures, read reliable works of theology, and listen to solid biblical teaching. We need a healthy dose of truth. But to correct a faulty emotional view of God, we need something else. We need to be "reparented." We need friends and mentors to show us in flesh-and-blood life how to see and relate to God. As we hang out with these fellows believers who have a healthy, biblical view of God, pretty soon it rubs off on us at a deep emotional level. We begin not only to know about God mentally but to experience his love and care emotionally.

God's Master Plan

The Christian life is a waiting life. We never stop waiting on the Lord. We wait on him for school plans, for a marriage partner, for a job. We wait on him during times of weakness as well as times of strength. We wait on him as we carry out the work he has given us, like enduring the rigors of grad school or finishing a big project. Being a godly parent involves waiting as we pray that our kids will grow into men and women who love God. Making disciples involves waiting. Planting and growing a church involves waiting. It seems as if we're always waiting, and that's not easy for people like us who live in an instant-gratification culture.

What helps us wait is knowing what we are waiting for. I'm not talking about what we are individually waiting for, but I mean what we as the people of God are waiting for. Why do we have to wait at all? What is God up to? What is God's master plan?

Before God made anything, Father, Son, and Spirit, the triune God, were living in the perfect community, each loving and serving the other. God didn't need to create human beings, but he's a giving God, so he did. A giving God wants to share the perfect community with his creation. But Satan and sin derailed the project for a time, and Revelation tells the story of how God will finish what he started back in Genesis. At the end of Revelation we read, "The Lord, the God who inspires the prophets, sent his angel to show his servants the things that must soon take place" (22:6). The phrase "things that must soon take place" refers to God's plan for his creation. God is basically saying, "I've got this."

In Revelation 5, John sees God seated on his throne and holding a scroll firmly in his right hand. The scroll represents God's plan to defeat evil once and for all, to rescue his people, and to transform his creation through the victory achieved by Jesus Christ, the Lamb of God. The rest of Revelation shows us how God will pull this off. The reappearance of the scroll in chapter 10 makes it clear (unfortunately) that God's plan may call us to suffer persecution as we follow Christ faithfully in a hostile world. Bearing witness to God's plan comes at a price.

God's grand purpose or plan can be traced back to a promise he made long ago, a promise with three parts: (1) I will be your God, (2) you will be my people, and (3) I will live among you (see the table).[10] The promise takes many shapes and sizes throughout the Scriptures (see the table). The fulfillment of this long-standing promise involves both a people and a place.

God's goal is to share the perfect community with his people in a whole new creation.

God's Promises of Community

Exodus 29:45–46	Then I will dwell among the Israelites and be their God. They will know that I am the LORD their God, who brought them out of Egypt so that I might dwell among them. I am the LORD their God.
Leviticus 26:11–12	I will put my dwelling place among you, and I will not abhor you. I will walk among you and be your God, and you will be my people.
Ezekiel 37:27	My dwelling place will be with them; I will be their God, and they will be my people.
Zechariah 2:10–11	"For I am coming, and I will live among you," declares the LORD. "Many nations will be joined with the LORD in that day and will become my people. I will live among you."
Revelation 21:3	And I heard a loud voice from the throne saying, "Look! God's dwelling place is now among the people, and he will dwell with them. They will be his people, and God himself will be with them and be their God."
Revelation 21:7	Those who are victorious will inherit all this, and I will be their God and they will be my children.

God has always wanted a people drawn from all the nations. The great multitude of Revelation 5 comes from "every tribe and language and people and nation" (5:9), and this fulfills God's original promise to Abraham that he would be the father of many nations (Gen 12:3; 15:5; 17:4). Cultural differences won't be destroyed in the new creation. Rather, they will be transformed into a symphony of praise to our Creator and Redeemer. This picture of believers drawn from many nations worshiping God reminds us that God created and loves all peoples. The multicultural reality of heaven calls us to be involved now in sharing the gospel with all peoples and embracing believers who are different from us. An authentically multicultural church offers the world a window into heaven and clearly reflects the master plan of God.

God's plan also involves a place for his people. He wants to live among us. There is really no place like home. Let it sink in that God really wants to make his home with us. In the Old Testament, God lived among his people in the form of a tabernacle and later a temple. Then Jesus Christ came to earth and "made his dwelling" (literally, "tabernacled") among us (John 1:14).[11] But God wants more than to occupy a building among us or even walk among us. He wants us to live with him in a whole new creation, a new heaven and new earth. Revelation 21–22 describes in some detail our new home in the presence of God. (We have a whole chapter on the new creation later in the book [see chap. 9].) For now, it's enough to know that God's plan is for us to be with him and to enjoy his presence forever.

Part of the Westminster Shorter Catechism says, "Man's chief end is to glorify God, and *to enjoy him forever.*"[12] Maybe we need to focus a bit more on this last line. If God has gone to this much trouble to make a whole new world for us, maybe we will become convinced that he wants to live in intimate fellowship with us . . . starting now. That is an important part of God's master plan.

God Wins!

Over the past several years, I've experienced the death of two of my students. I knew them well, and the loss hurt deeply. I hate death, and I'm glad the apostle Paul rightly has called it "the last enemy" (1 Cor 15:26). As long as death and sin and Satan and those who partner with them are still around, God's great plan will not be complete. Don't you find yourself at times crying out, "Come back, Lord, and fix this broken world; come back and make all things new"? What God began in Genesis and accomplished at the cross and resurrection of Jesus, he will now complete in Revelation. Spoiler alert: God wins!

Much of the book of Revelation is about God's judgment of evil. In chapters 6–16 there are three sets of judgments, each with seven parts: the seals, the trumpets, and the bowls. Since the numbers seven and three indicate completeness, three sets of seven tell us that God is going to fully and completely destroy evil. Then, in chapters 17–18, he judges Babylon the Great, a symbol for a center of pagan power. The early Christians referred to Rome as Babylon (1 Pet 5:13). In chapter 20 God condemns Satan, his demonic followers, and all wicked humans. Then finally, God condemns death: "Then death and Hades [the grave, or realm of the dead] were thrown into the lake of fire" (20:14). So much judgment. Is all this really necessary?

God's judgment of evil flows directly out of his covenant love for his people and his holy and righteous character. Before I explain how this shows up in Revelation, let me tell you a story. My wife, Judy, and I have three daughters. I remember a day when they were younger when one of the girls was home alone and a stranger began knocking on the front door. My daughter called me at school in a panic, saying that a strange man was trying to break into the house. I told her that I was sure that everything would be fine and suggested that she not answer the door. I suspected the solicitor would soon disappear when no one answered. About two minutes later she called again and said he was still knocking, louder this time. She was crying, and I was beginning to get worried. When she called the third time, I answered long enough to tell her I was on my way. I sped home, becoming angrier by the mile. I would not let this strange man harm my precious child. My confrontation with the (foolish and persistent) salesman wasn't exactly Christlike. I gave him an extra-hard handshake and may have even chest bumped him a bit before verbally confronting him about his stupid behavior. But I did learn something from the experience. I poured out my wrath on the salesman because he was (so I thought) threatening my daughter. My judgment against the salesman was the flip side of my deep love for my daughter. The same is true for God, except he always judges in a way that is just and right.

Again, God must judge evil because he loves us and because he is holy and righteous and cannot let evil win. To say that God is righteous is to say that he is totally committed to doing what is right, to acting in a way that is consistent with his holy character. The angels praise God as "holy, holy, holy" (4:8). The song of the redeemed in chapter 15 includes these lyrics: "Who will not fear you, Lord, and bring glory to your name? For you alone are holy" (15:4). In chapter 16, an angel calls out, "You are just in these judgments, O Holy One" (16:5). Over and over again in Revelation, we are told that God is righteous and holy. Because of who he is, he always judges justly rather than arbitrarily or randomly.

Many cringe at the thought of God condemning those who rebel against him. It seems, on the surface, to be mean and unloving. But I suspect that Christians living in places where fellow believers are murdered simply for naming the name of Christ would understand why God's judgment is necessary. Real evil exists in this world, and many of you have experienced it. God really loves you, and he will not allow evil to have the last word over you, his precious child.

In Revelation 6, the martyrs cry out, "How long, Sovereign Lord, holy and true, until you judge the inhabitants of the earth [the wicked] and avenge our blood?" (6:10). God tells them to wait a little while longer. God is patient (read 2 Pet 3:8–9 about why he is patient), but he will not let evil win. One day, he will condemn the wicked people and demonic powers who have hurt his children (e.g., Rev 11:18; 16:6; 18:20; 19:1–2). Evil will not win. God wins!

Conclusion

Revelation tells us that God is in control, that he is more powerful than all other gods, that he loves us deeply, that he has a plan to fix this broken world, and that he will defeat evil once and for all. We fail at life when we put ourselves or any other thing or person at the center. God Almighty is the true center and source of life.

Here is how God created life to work:

- God is the true center and source of life. He created us and loves us deeply (Rom 5:8).
- When we acknowledge God as the true center, we experience his love. Our core identity becomes "the disciple whom Jesus loved," and there is nothing more we can do to gain acceptance with God.
- Since we can trust God to always love and care for us, our need for love is met, and we are now free to love and care for others.
- When we give to others, God is deeply pleased and our life works in the best possible way. And since others will serve and give to us, we are also receiving human love as well, and this creates that wonderful thing known as biblical community.[13]

Life is way too fragile and fragmented for us to be our own center. That is the essence of sin. Revelation says God Almighty is the only true center. When we truly get that, our response is to fall on our faces in worship—the topic of our next chapter.

Key texts: Rev 1:4–8; 4:1–11; 11:17–18; 21:7
Reading plan: Revelation 1; 4

Community Group Questions

1. What do people seem to be turning to these days in an attempt to find a true center for their lives?
2. How does it help you to know that God is not just sovereign over the events of history but also more powerful than all the forces of evil?
3. If you have struggled to let God love you, what has helped you the most to receive and live in his love?
4. How does God's judgment of evil help you understand more about his love? Why is God's judgment of evil necessary?
5. Even as believers, we sometimes drift into thinking that we are the center of the universe. What leads us down that road?
6. How does trying to be our own true center actually make life much harder in the long run?
7. How can your community help you to trust God Almighty as the only true center?

2

WORSHIP
"You Are Worthy"

We were made to worship, and we will always find a way to worship something. Perhaps the question is, Will we worship the right something, or more accurately, the right someone? Revelation offers a huge dose of wisdom and encouragement to help us worship the one true God. Revelation calls us to reject idolatry in its many forms, but idolatry cannot be overcome by warnings and prohibitions alone. We are not made to say no to something without saying yes to something better. Instead, "idolatry must be replaced by worship."[1] Worship of the one true God has the power to liberate us from our idolatrous addictions precisely by replacing them.

We encounter objects of worship everywhere. In the fall of 2011, the Arkansas Razorbacks traveled to play a football game with the Louisiana State University Tigers, with a possible trip to the national championship game on the line. The Tigers' home stadium, known as "Death Valley," is a tough place for visiting teams to play because the fans are intense. At this particular game, one announcer spoke more than he knew

37

when he said, "Make no mistake: *worship happens here.*" As anyone who lives in the southeastern United States will tell you, passion for college football often looks like worship: hands raised, mental concentration, verbal participation, emotional involvement. More recently, I was watching a football game in late August between Texas A&M and South Carolina, when longtime announcer Brent Musburger made this comment: "As they say in these parts [the American South], college football is much more than just a religion, because it's much more important than that."[2] We were made to worship, and we will worship.

As the supreme worship book in the New Testament, perhaps the entire Bible, Revelation tells us that God alone is worthy of our worship. Our hearts are restless until they rest in the worship of the true God.[3] He alone can bear the weight of our adoration and affection. In the last chapter, we learned that God is in control, that he is King of kings, that he is our faithful Father, that he has a master plan, and that he will one day destroy evil. The only proper response to this kind of God is worship. As Eugene Peterson puts it, "Worship is an act of attention to the living God who rules, speaks and reveals, creates and redeems, orders and blesses."[4]

The big question in Revelation is whether people will worship God and the Lamb or the dragon and the beast. In 13:4 we read, "People worshiped the dragon because he had given authority to the beast, and they also worshiped the beast and asked, 'Who is like the beast? Who can wage war against it?'" In 15:4 we read, "Who will not fear you, Lord, and bring glory to your name? For you alone are holy. All nations will come and worship before you, for your righteous acts have been revealed." The same language of worship is used to describe both the worship of God and the worship of Satan. Worship stands at the very center of this cosmic conflict between God and the forces of evil. We were made to worship, and we will worship. In this chapter, we will see that Revelation has a lot to teach us about worship, and especially about the object of our worship.

Worship, the Heartbeat of Heaven

John received his vision that is the book of Revelation *while worshiping*: "On the Lord's Day I was in the Spirit, and I heard behind me a loud voice like a trumpet, which said: 'Write on a scroll what you see and send it to the seven churches'" (1:10–11). The early Christians designated Sunday, the first day of the week, as "the Lord's Day," a day of worship that honored the day Jesus was raised from the dead. Those who first listened to Revelation as it was read aloud did so in the setting of Spirit-guided worship (1:3). Gathering with other believers to worship remains one of the most significant things we do, because it's our way of imitating heaven. Worship is the business, the lifeblood, the heartbeat of heaven. Spirit-led worship here and now gives us a taste of heaven unlike anything else.

While I was traveling in Israel recently with a group of students from our university, we entered St. Anne's Church in Jerusalem. The building has amazing acoustics, and as we sang "How Deep the Father's Love for Us," the Holy Spirit welded our hearts together in a moment of deep, authentic praise. We could have stayed there all day. In those few minutes as we worshiped together, we became totally centered on our Lord, the true object of worship.

Just as Revelation opens with worship, so it also closes with worship. Chapter 21 reflects the permanence of heavenly worship as God's people begin living in his presence forever. And in chapter 22, God's people are said to "serve" him, a term that strongly suggests performing religious acts as a part of worship (see 7:15; 22:3).[5] Worship not only bookends Revelation; we see it repeated throughout in numerous scenes of worship: chapters 4–5; 7; 8; 11; 14; 15; 16; and 19.

Notice that the worship scenes of Revelation are all heavenly rather than earthly. The churches of chapters 2–3 were struggling in their worship, as we often struggle in ours. They were in a worship war that makes the battle between worship styles seem like kindergarten. Their war was about which God/god they would worship. That's why they needed to hear about how worship happens in the heavenly throne room. We do too! We need to see how it never stops. We need to see its purity and feel its power. We need to be reminded that worshiping our Lord is the most real thing that exists in all the universe. We need the heartbeat of heaven to empower our earthly worship and direct it to the only deserving object—our triune God.

We need a heavenly vision of true worship to liberate us from the idols that demand our attention and compete for our affections. We need to know why worship matters. We need to let Revelation's picture of worship open our eyes to see who God is, what he has done for us, and what he is going to do, because only a clear vision of God can produce passionate worship. That's why our worship leaders need to be not only competent musicians but also strong biblical theologians with pure hearts and sharp minds. Only as they know and love God can they lead us to see God clearly and worship him deeply.

Worship, a Response to God's Character

I'd always heard that being a grandparent was the best, but I didn't really pay much attention to it until Juliette, Hallie, and Emery came along and flipped our world upside down. I find myself delighting in our three granddaughters and their responses to me. It's pure joy when they give me a smile, a laugh, an inquisitive look, or a hug, or when they tell me a story or ask me a question.

As grandkids respond to grandparents when the relationship is good and healthy, genuine worship always involves our response to God. But before we can respond to God, we need to understand what kind of God he is. Even with our grand-daughters, I need to treat them gently, smile at them, talk to them, and care for them before they will respond positively to me. So it is with God. Once we know and feel how loving, beautiful, powerful, compassionate, holy, truthful, and giving God really is, we too will respond to him and love him back. That response of love constitutes the heart of worship.

I sometimes forget that worship is a response, and I fall into the trap of trying to ramp up my emotions to achieve worship. I enter the worship center, and we begin singing. The songs usually become more intense as we move through the worship set. Although I don't intentionally plan to "achieve worship," I get caught up in the moment and occasionally forget that I'm not responsible for "creating worship." Worship happens naturally when I center on God and respond to who God is and what he has done.

Revelation 4 reminds us that worship involves a response to who God is, to his character. Following John's vision of the seven churches in chapters 2–3, he is invited to heaven in chapter 4 for a very different vision: God in all his glory and brilliance, seated on his throne and surrounded by worshipers. This is the vision that centers and anchors all other visions throughout the book.

Two groups of angels—the four living creatures and the twenty-four elders—lead heaven to praise and glorify God. The creatures never stop saying, "'Holy, holy, holy is the Lord God Almighty,' who was, and is, and is to come" (4:8). They "give glory, honor and thanks to him who sits on the throne and who lives for ever and ever" (4:9). The elders fall down before God and cry out, "You are worthy, our Lord and God, to receive glory and honor and power, for you created all things, and by your will they were created and have their being" (4:11).

Revelation 4 shows God seated on his throne and reminds us that God is sovereign and majestic and glorious. He is light and lives in absolute splendor and brilliance (1 John 1:5; 1 Tim

6:16). In God there is no darkness at all. He is holy and pure and completely anti-evil. He is all-powerful and eternal. His purposes will be accomplished. And he is the Creator, meaning that he didn't keep his goodness to himself, but he created a world to share it with. As Creator, God is also the one who gives and sustains life.

Revelation 15 is similar to Revelation 4 in that the worshipers also respond with a song, this time the victorious song of Moses and the Lamb (15:3–4): "Great and marvelous are your deeds, Lord God Almighty. Just and true are your ways, King of the nations. Who will not fear you, Lord, and bring glory to your name? For you alone are holy. All nations will come and worship before you, for your righteous acts have been revealed." They praise God for being the sovereign, faithful ruler of the universe, who has condemned evil and saved his people. God alone is holy and righteous and worthy of glory and reverence. He deserves the praise of all peoples.

Because God is like this, you can trust him. You really can, knowing that there is not one ounce of evil in God, that he gave you life to begin with and will one day give you resurrection life, that he always does what is right, that he will never deceive or betray you, and that he has a plan to deliver you from evil and provide an eternal home for you in his presence. Your "thank you" is worship.

Worship, a Response to God's Mighty Acts

One of my seminary professors, Dr. Bert Dominy, used to say, "We know who God is by what he has done." (This is even true on a human level—we can tell the character of a person by his or her actions.) We worship God both for who he is *and* for what he does. The two go together. Revelation calls us to worship in response to God's mighty acts—past, present, and future.

God's first mighty act is creating. In Revelation 4 God is praised as the Creator: "You are worthy, our Lord and God, to receive glory and honor and power, for [or "because"] you created all things" (4:11). In 10:6 the mighty angel swears an oath by him who created the heavens, the earth, and the seas. In 14:7 an angel calls every nation, tribe, language, and people to "fear God and give him glory, because the hour of his judgment has come" and to "worship him who made the heavens, the earth, the sea and the springs of water."

To worship God as Creator is to admit that we are creatures. We owe our very existence to him. We wouldn't be here without him. He made us. We are totally dependent upon him. I'm not crazy about flying, and every time I get on an airplane, my prayer is the same: "Lord, my life is totally and completely in your hands." At that moment, I'm reminded that this is always true, whether I'm in the air or on the ground. My life is always in God's hands. He created me and sustains me. I owe my every breath and heartbeat to him. When I fly, however, I realize my complete dependence on God, because it brings me to a place of complete trust. There is absolutely nothing I can do to control my safety, except pray. To worship God as Creator calls forth total trust and dependence, and that's good.

Worshiping God as Creator also pulls us away from worshiping idols. All of us battle idolatry. Worship leader Bob Kauflin helps us understand that idolatry is a matter of displaced love:

> But we can't love anything in the right way unless we love God more. Our desires will be out of whack. We'll look to temporary pleasures like concerts, video games, and sports to fulfill eternal desires. We'll love things that aren't as worthy as God to be loved. How do I know what I love the most? By looking at my life outside of Sunday morning. What do I enjoy the most? What do I spend the most time doing? Where does my mind drift to when I don't have anything to do? What am I passionate about? What do I spend my money on? What makes me angry when I don't get it? What do I feel depressed without? What do I fear losing the most? Our answers to those questions will lead us straight to the God or gods we love and worship.[6]

43

The main difference between the one true God and idols is that we make idols, and the one true God made us. Only the Creator God is worthy of our worship.

It's mind-blowing to think that the God who once created will one day re-create. Just as God made the heavens and the earth (14:7), so he will make all things new (21:5). New Testament scholar Richard Bauckham writes, "Where faith in God the Creator wanes, so inevitably does hope for resurrection, let alone the new creation of all things. It is the God who is the Alpha who will also be the Omega."[7] Our future hope that God will make all things new comes from the reality of God as Creator. Our Maker can "remake" us after death.

Just as God is worshiped as Creator, so Jesus, the Lamb of God, is worshiped as Redeemer. Revelation 4 leads into Revelation 5, where the Lamb stands at the center of the throne and is surrounded by the living creatures and the elders (5:6). When he takes the scroll (the plan of God to destroy evil and save his people) from the Father, the angels go crazy in worship (5:7–10). They worship Jesus because he was slain on the cross, where he purchased for God people from every tribe, language, people, and nation.

The word for "purchase" (Gk. *agorazō*; 5:9) means to "redeem" or "buy back." In the ancient marketplace slaves were purchased, or redeemed, by their new owner. The early Christians felt this to be an appropriate word to describe what Jesus has done for us. Although we were slaves to sin and death, emptiness and hopelessness, Jesus paid with his very life to become our new owner and set us free. We have been purchased with the precious blood of Christ (14:3–4; cf. 1 Cor 6:19–20; 1 Pet 1:18–19). We worship Jesus our Redeemer for obeying the Father and going to the cross. In the garden of Gethsemane, when he saw there was no other way, he did what was right and good and necessary, rather than what was easy. He sacrificed himself to pay the price for our sins. He gave his life to give us life. Revelation 5 closes with millions of other angels and all of creation praising the Lamb, our Redeemer (5:11–14).

That's why it's comforting to hear that we have permission to worship God not only for what he has done but also for what he will do. Our worship doesn't just look back or look around; it also looks forward. We worship in anticipation of God's future mighty acts, even when our present circumstances seem unbearable.

The theme of worshiping God for what he is going to do runs throughout Revelation. Jesus is worshiped in chapter 5 for making God's people into a kingdom and priests, who will serve God and reign with him in the future. At the sounding of the seventh trumpet in chapter 11, loud heavenly voices announce that the "kingdom of the world has become the kingdom of our Lord and of his Messiah" (11:15), causing the twenty-four elders to worship God for beginning his eternal reign.

The greatest future mighty act of God is a lot more personal than we might imagine; it's actually a wedding. The image of marriage vividly showcases God's covenant love for his people and his desire to live with them forever. Revelation portrays Jesus as the Bridegroom and the church as the bride (19:7; 21:2, 9; 22:17). Chapter 19 shows that God is to be praised for bringing about the wedding of the Lamb and the church: "Hallelujah! For our Lord God Almighty reigns. Let us rejoice and be glad and give him glory! For the wedding of the Lamb has come, and his bride has made herself ready" (19:6–7).

I've been married to the same amazing woman since 1982, and it's been wonderful. A strong marriage is perhaps the best picture we have of the deep love relationship that God desires to have with us. But even when these relationships are at their absolute best, they are merely a drop in the ocean compared to God's infinite love for us. God has planned a beautiful, glorious future for us because he loves us and wants to be with us. This will be his final mighty act, and we worship him because of what he has promised to do.

THE HEART OF REVELATION

Worship, a Response to God's Victory over Evil

Have you ever found yourself cheering at the end of an epic movie when the good guys finally triumph over the bad guys, when good wins out over evil? Deep within us is the desire to see truth and justice prevail, to see right defeat wrong and good overcome evil. Perhaps surprisingly, one of the main reasons for worshiping God in Revelation is that he is the one who makes this happen.

When God begins his eternal reign, the elders fall down in worship and thank him for judging the wicked (11:17–18):

> We give thanks to you, Lord God Almighty, the One who is and who was, because you have taken your great power and have begun to reign. The nations were angry, and your wrath has come. The time has come for judging the dead, and for rewarding your servants the prophets and your people who revere your name, both great and small—and for destroying those who destroy the earth.

In Revelation 15 those who overcome are given harps and sing a new song, a song worshiping God for providing deliverance (15:3–4): "Great and marvelous are your deeds, Lord God Almighty. Just and true are your ways, King of the nations. Who will not fear you, Lord, and bring glory to your name? For you alone are holy. All nations will come and worship before you, for your righteous acts have been revealed." The celebration of God's people includes praise for conquering his enemies. God wins, and we praise him for the victory!

If this whole idea of praising God for destroying evil seems foreign or even distasteful to you, perhaps it's because most Christians in our culture don't face persecution. Only those familiar with the horrors of evil will find themselves prepared to praise God for deliverance from it.

God will judge evil, and his judgments are true and just (16:5–7). The forces of darkness will not win. They won't get away with harming God's beloved people. These forces deceive and manipulate and abuse and bring death all around, but not for long. Revelation gives us permission to praise God for being the kind of God who will destroy evil. Following the destruction of Babylon in chapter 18, a city symbolizing any great center of pagan power, God's people are commanded to rejoice that God has finally judged her: "Rejoice over her, you heavens! Rejoice, you people of God! Rejoice, apostles and prophets! For God has judged her with the judgment she imposed on you" (18:20). The command to rejoice in 18:20 prepares us for the hallelujah chorus that follows, where God's people "praise Yahweh" (Heb. *hallelu-jah*) for judging the wicked city (19:1–4):

> "*Hallelujah!* Salvation and glory and power belong to our God, for true and just are his judgments. He has condemned the great prostitute who corrupted the earth by her adulteries. He has avenged on her the blood of his servants." And again they shouted: "*Hallelujah!* The smoke from her goes up for ever and ever." The twenty-four elders and the four living creatures fell down and worshiped God, who was seated on the throne. And they cried: "Amen, *Hallelujah!*"

God deserves praise because his judgments flow out of his character as a faithful and righteous God (cf. 3:7; 15:3; 16:7). He has not excused or ignored evil, and he has not failed to rescue his suffering people. The cry of 6:10 has at last been answered: "How long, Sovereign Lord, holy and true, until you judge the inhabitants of the earth and avenge our blood?" (cf. 16:6–7; Ps 70:1). God's judgment of the adulterous and corrupting prostitute is just, decisive, and final (cf. Rev 14:11; Isa 34:8–10).

While worship means rejoicing when God defeats evil, this is not the same thing as satisfying a lust for revenge or delighting in the suffering of the wicked. God wants rebellious people to turn back to him, but they often refuse (see Rev 3:3, 19; 9:20–21; 16:9, 11). When people rebel, it breaks God's heart.

What is being celebrated here, however, is God's victory over evil and his faithfulness to his suffering people. God has finally answered their prayer for vindication (6:9–11). Evil will not win! And that is praiseworthy.

What kind of evil are you facing right now? Injustice, abuse, ridicule, addiction, disease, betrayal, or perhaps the death of someone you love? Part of your worship can be praising God that one day he will totally destroy all evil, once and for all.

Worship, a Holistic Response

Revelation not only tells us why to worship; it also tells us something about how we should worship. One of the most important words for "worship" in the book is the term for "falling down" (Gk. *proskyneō*). That's because in Revelation, as in the ancient world in general, worship involved a person's physical posture. Worship meant bowing or prostrating oneself before the object of worship to demonstrate humility and reverence. A couple of times John even falls down before angels, but the angels rebuke him and tell him to "worship God" instead (19:10; 22:8–9). In other words, the angels interpret John's falling down as worship.

Through our body language we tell everyone what we believe and how we feel about worshiping God. When I slouch or cross my arms, I distance myself from what is happening in the worship gathering. Others might indicate their individualistic beliefs about worship (all that matters is what I do) by spinning out of control emotionally with distracting bodily gestures. We send all sorts of signals through our body language. Revelation calls us to authentic and appropriate bodily worship that reflects a pure and authentic reverence for the Lord. We are worshiping the God of the universe, and kicking back as if we're listening to a boring lecture or watching a Sunday afternoon golf match simply won't do.

In both 2009 and 2016, I spent a month at Tyndale House in Cambridge, England. I worshiped regularly at Eden Baptist Church and loved it. During the first worship service at Eden, I was astounded that everyone sang with enthusiasm. Everyone. My experience in many American evangelical churches is that the singing is sporadic and lethargic. Not so in this British congregation. These Christians sang, all of them, as if they were outnumbered in their culture and desperately needed to gather each week with fellow believers and praise God with all their might.

Worship is more than singing, but in Revelation worship happens primarily through singing. There are numerous hymns (or portions of hymns) in Revelation: 4:8–11; 5:9–14; 7:10–12; 11:15–18; 12:10–12; 15:3–4; 16:5–7; 19:1–5, 6–8. These songs are always directed to God or Jesus Christ (or both) as expressions of worship. The singers include John, the four living creatures, the twenty-four elders, other angels, God's people, other heavenly voices, and all created beings. That includes pretty much everyone. The songs are sung, spoken, or shouted and are accompanied by falling down, crying out, or playing instruments. The songs take many forms: doxology, acclamation, amen, victory hymn, thanksgiving, and praise. They celebrate the character (e.g., holiness, glory, power, strength, wisdom) and mighty acts (creating, being slain, bringing salvation, judging, rewarding, defeating evil) of God and the Lamb.[8]

When we sing in worship, we confess our faith in God, who he is, and all that he has done. We also confess our hope in God and all that he is going to do. Worship through singing reminds us of what we believe. It focuses our attention and centers our affections on what really matters. It carries us through hard times. It shapes and strengthens us. It replaces fear with trust. It drives away the darkness and the demonic. It allows us to go on living. When we sing praises to our Lord, we speak the language of heaven.

Conclusion

In the Roman Empire, people sang praises to the Roman emperor, but the music used to worship the emperor can't compare to the worship of the one true God portrayed in Revelation. Worship is our most intimate and sacred response to God's character and actions. When many other important things have stopped, worship will still be going strong . . . for all eternity.

Revelation tells us five main things about worship. First, worship is the heartbeat of heaven. When Revelation describes heaven, it usually focuses on worship as the primary activity of heaven. Second, we are to worship God because of who he is. God is God, the holy and sovereign Creator and center of the universe. He alone deserves our worship. Third, we worship God not just for who he is but also for what he has done and what he will do for us. Fourth, we worship God for judging and destroying evil. Somewhat surprisingly, this aspect of worship stands strong in Revelation. Fifth, worship calls for a holistic response on our part, complete with appropriate attitudes (like fearing the Lord) and actions (like singing and bowing). Since we were made to worship and since we will worship, we need Revelation to help us get it right.

The bottom line is that worship means telling God how much we love him and how we recognize him as the true center of all reality. When we fail to worship, we become distracted, frightened, restless, selfish people susceptible to the powers of this world. In worship, everything is made right and whole again. We are put in our proper place as beloved creatures, no longer attempting to occupy the center. When we worship, we find that we are who we were made to be, and our restlessness stops as we come to find our rest in God alone.

Key texts: Rev 4:11; 5:9–14; 11:15–19; 19:1–8
Reading plan: Revelation 15; 19

Community Group Questions

1. What is your favorite definition of worship? How does what you read about worship in Revelation enhance your understanding of worship?

2. I mention in this chapter how we seem to worship sports. What are some other unworthy objects of worship in our culture?

3. Does it excite you or unnerve you that worship is the heartbeat of heaven? In other words, do you think we will be singing hymns for eternity? Why or why not?

4. What is your response to this statement: "The quality of our worship now ultimately goes back to the clarity of our vision of God"?

5. How does it deepen your worship to know that we worship God for who he is and for what he has done and for what he will do?

6. What do you think of Revelation making a big deal of praising God for defeating evil?

7. What does your body language say about what you believe about worship? What would help you (and your friends) to be more authentically enthusiastic in your worship?

3

THE PEOPLE OF GOD

"His Called, Chosen and Faithful Followers"

John had been exiled to the tiny island of Patmos by the Roman government for being a faithful witness to Jesus Christ (Rev 1:9). I've been to Patmos, and it's a pretty small place in the middle of a pretty big ocean, so I could see how John might feel isolated and useless. Nevertheless, he was faithfully worshiping one Sunday, when a trumpetlike voice told him to write on a scroll what he was about to see and send it to seven churches in Asia Minor. This series of visions became the book of Revelation. Notice also that the visions were meant primarily for the churches and not just for John. He was God's prophetic instrument to get the message out to the churches. And the number seven (symbolizing completeness in Revelation) tells us that these churches in some way represent all churches. The vision that is the book of Revelation is for all of God's people.

One of the reasons why God wants his people to under-stand this book is because it has so much to say about us. In

Revelation, Christians are called by dozens of different names, including servants, priests, brothers, partners in tribulation, church(es), faithful witnesses, saints, those who are sealed, the 144,000, the great multitude, those who follow the Lamb, firstfruits, my people, and the bride. There is not another book in the Bible that has so much to say about the people of God. Learning more about this particular theme invites us to take a good look in the spiritual mirror and search our own hearts to answer the question, Who are we as God's people, and how are we supposed to live in this world?

Everyone Struggles, Many Stay Faithful

Contrary to our idealistic picture of the early church, not a single congregation was perfect, and each had its own challenges and struggles. They were people, just like us. In John's vision in Revelation 1, he sees Jesus walking among the seven lampstands, which are identified as the seven churches. Jesus praises and commends most of the churches, but not all. He also accuses and warns many of the churches about their sin. These believers, like believers today, had issues. Their love was growing cold. They were caving in to idolatry and sexual immorality. They were buying into false teaching and were acting like hypocrites. They were infected with the spiritual virus known as apathy. I know it doesn't sound like the early church we've always heard about, but these are facts from the lips of Jesus himself. (Although John is the author of Revelation, he records the words of Jesus in 1:17–3:22.) Many of these believers were struggling to stay faithful.

The people of God have always been tempted by the dark side. We're in a spiritual battle. Everyone struggles. We're tempted to give in to the world mostly because it promises security and pleasure and power. We're also pressured and even threatened by the powerful leaders and systems of this world. Temptation is not only a lure to self-gratification; it's also a dangerous trap. Once a person sells his soul to any kind of earthly empire, that empire will not remain faithful to him. It will eventually turn on him and attempt to use him.

Babylon, the center of pagan power, stands guilty of four specific sins: (1) rejecting God through idolatry, (2) promoting sexual immorality, (3) using other people and nations to produce economic prosperity for herself, and (4) abusing (and even murdering) those who follow Jesus Christ (see 17:1–6).

Why would any Christian want to side with Babylon, the power that seduces and eventually abuses him? Good question, but it happened then and continues to happen now. It's a mystery as to why human beings sometimes cooperate with powers that will eventually bring them harm. The short answer is that we live in a broken world, and our enemies are very deceptive and seductive. Sin is basically falling for a lie, the lie that whatever is promised by these seductive powers is better than what God has provided and promised. Yes, sin is stupid.

In Rev 18:4 the heavenly voice calls out this command: "Come out of her [Babylon], my people, so that you will not share in her sins, so that you will not receive any of her plagues [or judgments from God]." The prophet Jeremiah said something very similar many years earlier: "Come out of her [Babylon], my people! Run for your lives! Run from the fierce anger of the LORD" (Jer 51:45). While obeying this command may involve physical separation, spiritual separation is more likely what is being called for. This command to separate from Babylon, the center of pagan power, sums up our call to holiness: a separation *from* the wicked ways of this world and a separation *unto* our God in loyalty and obedience.

We are a struggling people. We struggle to separate from worshiping false gods, like sports and entertainment and money. We struggle to avoid sexual immorality. We struggle not to use people to satisfy ourselves and amass wealth. We struggle to live in community with other Christians without damaging them in some way. Like the first Christians, we're a mess. But thankfully that is not the whole story. Many of us, dare I say most of us, will stay faithful to Jesus.

Don't miss how much Jesus praises the seven churches in Revelation 2–3. He commends them for their hard work of maintaining doctrinal purity, for enduring persecution (e.g., poverty, slander, imprisonment), for staying faithful in their witness in a secular environment, and for growing in their service, among other things.

In Revelation true believers are actually defined by their faithfulness: the people of God are "those who keep God's commands and hold fast their testimony about Jesus" (12:17) and "who keep his commands and remain faithful to Jesus" (14:12). The only named martyr in the book, Antipas, is described as "my faithful witness" by Jesus himself, the ultimate faithful witness (2:13). In chapter 6, with the opening of the fifth seal judgment, John sees under the heavenly altar the souls of those who have been slain because of the word of God and their testimony (6:9; cf. 20:4). They are waiting on God to judge their persecutors. John himself is one of many faithful people (1:9; 19:10; 22:9). In the end, the Lamb will triumph over his enemies and will be accompanied by his people—"his called, chosen and *faithful* followers" (17:14). In a nutshell, God's people "follow the Lamb wherever he goes" (14:4).

Many will stay faithful, but faithfulness doesn't come automatically. We will always feel the tension between giving in to temptation and remaining loyal to Jesus. We see the very same tension throughout Revelation. That's why at the end of all seven messages, Jesus makes promises to those who are victorious. We have a choice about whether or not we will stay the course and overcome. The term for "be victorious" (Gk. *nikaō*, meaning "overcome" or "conquer") would have been very familiar to the original audience. The Greek goddess Nike was the goddess of victory. The goddess is often pictured on coins or stone reliefs as a winged lady in flight, holding a palm branch and a wreath, both symbols of victory.[1] In Revelation, to be victorious means to stay faithful, not to win a competition. To be a Nike Christian is to be a faithful Christian.

So the name of the game is endurance, or perseverance. The Greek word from which we get our word "endurance" (Gk. *hypomonē*), which occurs seven times in Revelation (1:9; 2:2, 3, 19; 3:10; 13:10; 14:12), gets to the heart of our calling.[2] We must, by the grace of God, keep running the race. And it's not a 100-meter sprint; it's an ultramarathon.

The recipe for overcoming or conquering is found in 12:11: "They triumphed [same Greek word for "be victorious," *nikaō*] over him by the blood of the Lamb and by the word of their testimony; they did not love their lives so much as to shrink from death." We conquer the powers of darkness by trusting in Christ's sacrifice on the cross and by staying faithful in our witness to Christ even in the face of suffering or death. To overcome is to follow the Lamb with one's whole life until the very end of one's life.

A Persecuted but Protected People

Sometimes we Christians are annoying and self-absorbed and deserve the ridicule we receive from unbelievers. In which case, opposition has nothing to do with our relationship to Jesus. We're just being obnoxious, hard-to-get-along-with people. At other times, the story is much different. When Revelation was written, Christians were facing pressure to conform to an ungodly empire or face the consequences of exclusion, economic deprivation, imprisonment, or death. At that time, Christians were experiencing pressure from local authorities to honor the Roman emperor in ways that amounted to worship. Yet, participating in such activities contradicted the most basic Christian confession: "Jesus is Lord" (cf. 2:13; 17:6; 18:24; 19:2). Those who refused to join in usually faced persecution of a social and economic (and perhaps a physical) nature. There are also general references in Revelation to God's people experiencing trouble and opposition, but the source is not named (e.g., 1:9; 2:3; 6:9–10; 16:6; 20:4). Revelation leaves us with the impression that the situation for those first believers wasn't good and was about to get much worse (3:10; 6:11; 12:11; 13:7, 10, 15).

Christians in some parts of the world today face pressure and opposition similar to that faced by the early church. According to Paul Marshall, Lela Gilbert, and Nina Shea, authors of the important book *Persecuted: The Global Assault on Christians*, "Christians are the single most widely persecuted religious group in the world today."[3] To be more specific, in many places people are prohibited from doing the following things (a sample list):

- converting to Christianity
- assembling for peaceful religious activities such as worship, preaching, or prayer
- speaking freely about Christian beliefs
- possessing or giving out religious literature, including Bibles
- teaching their children to follow Jesus

If you are caught doing any of these things, you could be detained, interrogated, fined, put in a labor camp or prison, resettled, tortured, enslaved, or executed.

This begs the question, why does the world hate the church? Revelation 12 answers this question. In chapter 12, a woman gives birth to a male child (Jesus). The woman is probably not Mary, the mother of Jesus, because in 12:17 we read about the "rest of her offspring," an expression referring to a whole group of people. The woman likely represents the community of God's people that gave birth to the Messiah, Jesus Christ. As the story continues, a red dragon (Satan) attempts to destroy the child at his birth but is unsuccessful. The child is protected and eventually ascends to God and his throne. (The story assumes, but doesn't describe, the life, death, and resurrection of Jesus.) Meanwhile, there is a battle in heaven: Michael the archangel defeats Satan, who is now cast down to earth. While the heavens rejoice at the downfall of Satan, the earth mourns because now God's people face a furious and wounded enemy. Since Satan has failed to destroy the male child Jesus, he turns his full anger against the rest of the woman's offspring (v. 17)—those who keep God's commands and stay faithful to Jesus (i.e., the church). So, we see in Revelation 12 that the world hates the church because we are followers of Jesus, engaged in spiritual warfare with the devil, the prince of this world (John 12:31; 16:11).

That sounds ominous, but the really good news is that we don't have to live in fear of our spiritual enemies or of God's judgment they will receive. We may be a persecuted people, but we are also a protected people. Revelation 6 closes with a warning about the coming wrath of God and the Lamb and the question, "For the great day of their wrath has come, and who can withstand it?" (6:17). Revelation 7 answers this question: only those who have the seal of the living God can withstand the outpouring of God's wrath against evil. Believers may suffer persecution, but they will never, ever suffer the wrath of God. As the apostle Paul puts it, "There is now no condemnation [God's wrath or judgment] for those who are in Christ Jesus" (Rom 8:1).

In Revelation 7 God gives his servants (all believers) the "seal of the living God" (7:2–8). In the ancient world scrolls were rolled up, tied, and sealed using a signet ring to make an impression on a clump of wax that held a string in place. This stamped seal showed that the document was genuine, that it truly belonged to the owner/sender, and that the message it contained was legally authentic. By sealing his people with his Spirit (see 2 Cor 1:22; Eph 1:13; 4:30), God has promised to protect us. He has stamped or marked us with his seal of ownership. We are truly his people, and nothing can separate us from our Lord.

Here is what all this means. God has never promised to protect us from physical persecution or suffering, but he has promised that we will never experience his wrath or condemnation. He has sealed us against spiritual defeat at the hands of the evil one. We are empowered by God's Spirit to remain loyal to Christ to the very end. We don't have to fear Satan or the demonic or evil in general. As it says in 1 John 4:4, "The one who is in you [the Holy Spirit] is greater than the one who is in the world [Satan]." Even on those days when doubts and fears assault us, we can know that we belong to Christ and that God has sealed us for eternity. God the Spirit is our personal guarantee that God will finish what he started in us (2 Cor 5:5; Eph 1:14). During times of intense spiritual struggle, we can know that we belong to God and that he will protect us until the day Jesus returns to claim us (Phil 1:6). We are called to overcome, but our perseverance is rooted in the grace of God made real in our lives through the power of the Holy Spirit, the seal of the living God. We are persecuted but protected.

A People with a Prophetic Mission

When we read in Revelation about Christians suffering and hear about the persecuted church today, it can make us want to run and hide until Jesus returns. It's true, we will never get into trouble if we don't say anything controversial or take a stand for God's unpopular truth. We could play it safe, never offend anyone with our Christian faith, and stay out of trouble. But the words of Jesus in Luke 6:26 have always haunted me when it comes to this sort of thing: "Woe to you when everyone speaks well of you, for that is how their ancestors treated the false prophets." Jesus's words can easily be taken out of context, and we have to be careful not to do that. But Revelation makes one thing clear: God's people are not called to cower and hide and retreat and play it safe all

60

the time. God has given us a mission that calls for boldness and courage.

God's mission for his people is to bear witness to his saving story, a story that centers on the life, death, and resurrection of Jesus Christ and finishes with the rescue of a people, the total destruction of evil, and the renewal of creation. Revelation 11 speaks of two witnesses who play a crucial role in the mission. This chapter is perhaps the most complicated in the entire book to interpret, but the gist of it is that the two witnesses represent the witnessing church.[4] The task of these witnesses is to live and speak God's truth boldly and clearly, as did the prophets of old. God gives them power and authority to fulfill their mission. They are spiritually protected but not exempted from persecution and even martyrdom as they carry out their mission. In the end, not even death can defeat the witnesses since God is the God of the living and raises them from the dead.

Today the word "martyr" refers to dying in the cause of Christ, but at the time Revelation was written, the Greek words *martyria* and *martys* simply meant "witness" or "testimony." This group of words is connected in Revelation with Christians dying for their faith (e.g., 2:13; 17:6). In other words, staying faithful to Jesus is directly related to being a faithful witness, and being a faithful witness lies at the heart of our God-given mission.

There are an almost infinite number of "Christian" causes we can become passionate about, and many of these fall in line with our mission of living and telling God's story. But some are distractions and detours that take us away from the mission. We have to ask ourselves some important questions from time to time: In all that I'm doing, am I really focusing on our God-given mission? Are there good things that are causing me to lose sight of the main thing? How can I become even more engaged in living and telling God's story? Do I expect to suffer when I act courageously to carry out the mission? Am I relying on God's strength and power as I live missionally?

Several years ago, I read Laura Hillenbrand's *New York Times* bestselling book *Unbroken*, the story of Louis Zamperini, an Olympic athlete and World War II hero, who suffered tremendously both adrift at sea after being shot down and later in a Japanese prison camp. The later movie by the same name, directed by Angelina Jolie, is good but doesn't tell the whole story. After the war, Zamperini battled bitterness toward his captors, nightmares, alcoholism, a violent temper, and a failing marriage. In 1949, his wife, Cynthia, attended the Billy Graham Crusade in Los Angeles, where she heard the gospel and came to Christ. She had prepared divorce papers, and after her conversion she tore them up and persuaded Louis to attend the same crusade. The first time Louis heard Graham preach, he walked out. But a few days later, Louis returned and heard the gospel clearly proclaimed and gave his heart to Christ. His life changed: the nightmares, the alcoholism, the temper, the anger, the strained relationships—all melted away, and he started to live for Christ. He even made efforts to reconcile with his Japanese persecutors. Louis Zamperini and his wife were changed by the good news faithfully preached by Graham. As a minister of the gospel, Billy Graham never lost sight of his main mission: to live and tell the story of Jesus Christ.

God has called us to join him in this mission, because God loves people and wants more of them to spend forever with him. Throughout Revelation, the nations receive God's offer of salvation. While many reject his offer and face judgment, some nations respond positively and enter God's kingdom (5:9; 7:9; 15:4; 21:24–26; 22:2). The Great Commission is Jesus calling his people to join him in making disciples of all nations (Matt 28:18–20). The Holy Spirit empowers us to live and tell God's story all because God loves the nations. Jesus came "to seek and to save the lost" (Luke 19:10). May we care more and more about people who desperately need a relationship with their Creator God.

Multicultural Multitude Bound for Paradise in God's Presence

One of the biggest lies being thrown at the American church today is the notion that Christians living in the last days will get to avoid any kind of persecution or tribulation. We get this idea from popular novels and Hollywood rather than from the book of Revelation, which makes it crystal clear that Christians will face such things.[5] The last days actually began with Jesus, and Christians have experienced persecution from that time forward. But in the same breath, Revelation also speaks of something better for God's people. Suffering is not the final chapter in God's great story. Much like God's people in the Old Testament, we have been liberated from slavery, and we're now on a long journey through the wilderness, anticipating our final destination in the heavenly promised land.

Before we get to the promised land part, it's cool to see who is traveling with us on this long pilgrimage. God's people come from all over the world. In Revelation 5 we meet a phrase that appears seven times in the book, arranged in a different order every time: "persons from every tribe and language and people and nation" (5:9; cf. 7:9; 10:11; 11:9; 13:7; 14:6; 17:15). This phrase doesn't always refer to true believers (11:9; 13:7; 17:15), but it does always indicate universality, showing that the group includes many different types of people. When it does refer to followers of Christ, as in 5:9 and 7:9, it shows that God has always wanted his people to come from all the peoples of the world. In other words, God has always desired a multicultural people. He longs to receive worship from all peoples and nations and languages and tribes. After all, he created them in the first place and certainly wants to save them, if they will only let him.

Have you ever heard Christians worshiping in a language you didn't understand? One vivid memory for me was a trip to a small town in Nicaragua, where I taught the Bible to pastors from the surrounding region. During that week I taught through a translator and felt pretty good about the teaching.

But the highlight was not my teaching. Rather, it was their singing. I know very little Spanish, but that didn't matter. Their enthusiastic worship moved me deeply. It also reminded me that the body of Christ is big, really big—much bigger than my church or state or nation or race or language or even my time in history.

Revelation 7 shows a "great multitude" standing before God and the Lamb in heaven, following their tribulation on earth. In 7:1–8 we see God's people sealed or protected and prepared for spiritual battle. Then in 7:9–17 we see the same group from a different perspective. Here they are celebrating their victory. The great multitude is drawn from every people group, fulfilling God's promised blessings to Abraham (Gen 15:5–6; 16:10; 17:4; cf. Gal 3:6–8). God has always wanted a people drawn from all the peoples of the world.

Does it surprise you to learn that cultural distinctives are not destroyed in heaven? Instead, they are transformed into an orchestra of praise to our Creator and Redeemer. The multitude is praising God for saving them and bringing them safely into his heavenly presence. We are told that God will "shelter" or "tabernacle over" them. This recalls God's protection and guidance of his people during their wilderness journey from slavery in Egypt to the promised land by covering them with his Shekinah, the glorious and radiant presence of God dwelling among his people (e.g., Exod 40:34–38).

Revelation 21–22 develops this theme of living in God's presence in much greater detail. One of the most comforting sections of the whole Bible is Rev 21:1–7:

> Then I saw "a new heaven and a new earth," for the first heaven and the first earth had passed away, and there was no longer any sea. I saw the Holy City, the new Jerusalem, coming down out of heaven from God, prepared as a bride

beautifully dressed for her husband. And I heard a loud voice from the throne saying, "Look! God's dwelling place is now among the people, and he will dwell with them. They will be his people, and God himself will be with them and be their God. 'He will wipe every tear from their eyes. There will be no more death' or mourning or crying or pain, for the old order of things has passed away." He who was seated on the throne said, "I am making everything new!" Then he said, "Write this down, for these words are trustworthy and true." He said to me: "It is done. I am the Alpha and the Omega, the Beginning and the End. To the thirsty I will give water without cost from the spring of the water of life. Those who are victorious will inherit all this, and I will be their God and they will be my children."

God's people have a wonderfully bright future. What God began in Genesis 1–2, which got messed up by Satan and sin, is now made complete at the end of Revelation. This will include a whole new world without any of the bad stuff—"'no more death' or mourning or crying or pain." Everything will be totally new. God himself will wipe away our tears, and we will enjoy his loving presence and his abundant provisions forever. The message of Revelation can be summed up using the apostle Paul's words: "Our present sufferings are not worth comparing with the glory that will be revealed in us" (Rom 8:18).

Conclusion

Have you ever noticed how almost everyone wants to be part of a group? The old sitcoms that ran for multiple seasons, such as *Cheers* or *Friends* or *Seinfeld*, focused on communities. We were created for community. I'm an introvert, and on a scale of one to ten, with one being an extreme introvert, I'm probably a two, maybe a three, but even I need community. Life was meant to be lived in community.

Revelation reminds us that God has created a community, the church, that exceeds all the friendships of the American classic sitcoms. In the book we learn many things about the community of Christ. In the messages to the seven churches in Revelation 2–3, we see people who are strongly tempted to compromise with the world. It's easier and safer to go along with those in charge of this world than to be faithful to Jesus, but this works only in the short run. We read of many churches that do stay faithful to Jesus and about how God plans to reward them. Revelation also encourages us to remember that we're not alone in this struggle. We're part of a great multitude of people who are staying true to Jesus in spite of the difficulty of persevering.

Revelation also helps us adjust our expectations. Many Christians in the West today do not expect to have to suffer for the cause of Christ in any way. But the first followers of Jesus suffered persecution, and God's people have suffered opposition and even martyrdom throughout history. Why should we expect anything different? On the night before he went to the cross, Jesus told his disciples: "In this world you will have trouble [the Greek word for "tribulation," *thlipsis*]. But take heart! I have overcome the world" (John 16:33). But we must keep in mind that there is a huge difference between the suffering dealt out by the world and the wrath of God. Believers will *never* experience the wrath of God, because Jesus has already taken our judgment through his death on the cross. We have been sealed or protected by God from all spiritual harm. We can live fearlessly in the protective love of God.

Revelation also reminds us that we have important work to do and an amazing future to anticipate. God wants to rescue people, and he calls us to assist him in getting the word out about his offer. Our mission is to live and speak God's great story of rescue. The message is for all peoples. Everyone needs to know that God will win. Satan and sin have temporarily hindered God's desire to live among his people in a beautiful world, but that interruption will end. One day God will make all things new and destroy all the evil that threatens us. We will then experience the unhindered presence of God, where we will find total healing and the absence of all evil. We will be constantly sheltered by God's loving, glorious presence and live in total security, peace, and joy.

God didn't have to create us, but he did. And Jesus didn't have to save us, but he did. And the Holy Spirit doesn't have to walk with us on this perilous but exciting journey to the new Jerusalem, but he does. Revelation reminds us that being a member of God's covenant community is one of life's greatest privileges.

Key texts: Rev 5:9; 12:17; 21:1–7
Reading plan: Revelation 2–3; 21

Community Group Questions

1. Read Revelation 2:9–10 about the experience of the church at Smyrna. Do you, deep down, expect to suffer like those believers? What is shaping your expectations about suffering or not suffering?

2. What do you think about God's strategy of spiritual protection through tribulation rather than physical immunity from it?

3. How can you know more about the persecuted church around the world today? What should we be praying for our fellow believers who are suffering?

4. What is the difference between persecution and God's wrath?

5. So much of what we do as Christians seems unrelated to our God-given mission of living and telling his story. How can we begin to change that?

THE HEART OF REVELATION

6. Read Revelation 22:17. Although the return of Christ is stressed throughout the book, the immediate context suggests that it is better to interpret all four commands of verse 17 ("come" and "take") as invitations to the hearers to respond positively to Christ rather than as calls for Christ to return. How does this emphasize our mission even more?

7. We have a whole chapter on the new heaven and the new earth later in the book, but what do you look forward to the most about life in the new creation?

4

THE HOLY SPIRIT

"The Seven Spirits before His Throne"

Perhaps you've sung the old hymn "Holy, Holy, Holy," which finishes with these words: "God in three persons, blessed Trinity." Throughout Revelation you will read about God Almighty and Jesus, the Lamb of God, but you won't read much about the Holy Spirit. Or so it seems. The Holy Spirit has been rightly referred to as the "shy member of the Trinity."[1] This is not a shyness of embarrassment or timidity but a shyness of humility, of being others-centered. The Spirit's mission is not to draw attention to himself but to point people to Jesus, and while not as conspicuous as the Father and the Son, the Spirit plays a surprisingly significant role in the book of Revelation (see also John 14:26; 15:26; 16:13–14).

In everyday life, we experience how something less prominent can still be vital. For instance, when you are driving a car, you probably focus on having enough gas in the tank, keeping a comfortable temperature, finding the right radio station, and having your mirrors adjusted properly, but I doubt you pay much, if any, attention to the tires. Last time I had my oil changed, the attendant mentioned that one of my tires only had 15 pounds of pressure (25–30 is normal). But "where the rubber meets the road" is 100 percent important and essential to how well your car drives, or if it even drives at all. No tires or even bad tires, and nothing else matters. You won't be driving very far. I'm not really comparing the Spirit to a set of new tires, but I am comparing a "shy" but critical component of an automobile with the less noticeable but fundamentally significant role of the Holy Spirit. In this chapter, you'll see how the Holy Spirit plays a crucial role in the book of Revelation.

The Seven Spirits: God's Powerful Presence in the World

To begin with, we see a thinly veiled reference to the Spirit in the book's opening greeting (1:4–5): "Grace and peace to you from him who is, and who was, and who is to come, and from the seven spirits before his throne, and from Jesus Christ, who is the faithful witness, the firstborn from the dead, and the ruler of the kings of the earth." This is a greeting from the triune God: Father ("him who is, and who was, and who is to come"), Spirit ("the seven spirits before his throne"), and Son ("Jesus Christ"). God's Spirit is the one who reaches into our lives with grace and peace from the Father and the Son.

Why does John refer to the Spirit as "the seven spirits before his throne"? It seems to be a strange way to speak about the Spirit, but the symbolism makes it come alive. "Before the throne" is simply the place where God's might and power are made known, the place where God connects directly with the world, you might say. Interestingly, the phrase "seven spirits" occurs four times in the book (1:4; 3:1; 4:5; 5:6). In Revelation, the number four represents creation, and the number seven represents completeness.[2] "Seven spirits," then, stands for God's full and complete power and action throughout creation, and this is the role of God's Spirit. God extends himself by his Spirit to act in this world.

Of these four places where "seven spirits" is used, in 1:4 the phrase refers to the Holy Spirit as a member of the Trinity. In 3:1, Jesus as the sovereign Lord holds the "seven spirits of God" and speaks to the church at Sardis. This church desperately needed to experience the reviving power of the Spirit of Christ. Only Jesus's power and sovereignty, made available through the Holy Spirit, can revive those on the verge of death. In front of the throne, in 4:5, are the seven lamps blazing, which are the "seven spirits of God." In 5:6, the Lamb has seven eyes, which are the "seven spirits of God sent out into all the earth."

The background of the phrase "seven spirits" is the Old Testament book of Zechariah, where we are told about the "seven eyes of the LORD that range throughout the earth" (Zech 4:10), and possibly Isa 11:1–10. Most important, we learn from Zechariah how God works in this world: "'Not by might nor by power, but by my Spirit,' says the LORD Almighty" (Zech 4:6). You might think of the Holy Spirit as the eyes and presence of God in the world, watching over his creation, walking with and convicting his people, and fighting against evil.

While the Father is in heaven, seated on his throne, and the Son has won the victory on earth but now shares the Father's throne in heaven, the Holy Spirit continues God's work on earth. The Father and the Son continue to work in the world through the Spirit.

Because we live in a society where technology and progress play such huge roles, I sometimes forget that God doesn't depend on human power or cleverness or intelligence to accomplish his work. He works by his Spirit. The most difficult thing to change in this world is a human heart, and that is the Holy Spirit's specialty as he convicts and prompts and leads. Here's a simple question: As you seek to do God's will in your life, do you sometimes slip into trying to do God's work apart from the power of the Spirit? It's generally good to be better organized and more efficient and more knowledgeable and better educated and more relevant and so forth. But unless we are crying out for the Spirit to work and watching for him to work and trusting him to work and cooperating with him as he works, we won't see the things happen that God wants to happen. Things might run more smoothly, and people might even be impressed, but a genuine work of God never occurs apart from the Spirit.

The night before Jesus went to the cross, he told his disciples to expect great things when the Spirit came at Pentecost (see John 14:26; 15:26; 16:7–15). With the coming of the Spirit (see the book of Acts), God's people were empowered to participate in God's mission in this world. At the very end of Revelation, in the closing section we read these words: "The Spirit and the bride say, 'Come!' And let the one who hears say, 'Come!' Let the one who is thirsty come; and let the one who wishes take the free gift of the water of life" (22:17). When I first heard those words, I thought they were a prayer for Christ to return (and they could be interpreted this way). While that is an important theme of Revelation, this verse seems to be saying something different. Both the bride and the Spirit say to those who hear, to those who thirst for the water of life: "Come" to Jesus. The Spirit is not crying out for Christ to return but instead pleading with those who need life to come to Jesus and take the free gift of living water. The Spirit also gives us the strength and power to join him in inviting people to come to Christ to find life. The bride also says, "Come." How amazing it is that God has put his Spirit within us to strengthen us to do his work in this world! But we have to learn to listen to the voice of the Spirit.

Listen to What the Spirit Says to the Churches

In any relationship, communication is crucial. Whether it's a friendship or a work situation or a marriage, for the relationship to be healthy you have to both listen to each other and talk to each other—to understand and be understood. The same is true for our relationship with God. We have to communicate in order to have a healthy relationship. Thankfully, the Holy Spirit is the Spirit of the Word, who speaks to God's people. Our job is to listen.

We see the Spirit speaking in Revelation first through the way he gives the visions to John and inspires the prophecy that became the book of Revelation. John is said to be "in the Spirit" four times in Revelation, and on each occasion John receives a heavenly vision (1:10; 4:2; 17:3; 21:10). In 1:10, he's worshiping God when the Spirit gives him the vision of Revelation. After John hears about the struggling churches in chapters 2–3, he is lifted up to heaven in a second vision to see the center of all reality in chapters 4–5: heaven praising God on his throne and the Lamb, who alone is worthy to carry out God's plan. In chapter 17, the Spirit continues the vision by showing John how God will judge the great prostitute, Babylon. In other words, God is telling us that he plans to destroy evil and warns us not to participate in wickedness. In 21:10, the Spirit shows John a very different woman/city—the bride of Christ, or new Jerusalem. It's almost as if John gets to see the bride of Christ, the church, walking down the aisle to meet her husband.

The Spirit inspires and breathes out these visions to reveal God's heart and his plans. Through these visions God is speaking to his people, telling them not to flirt with the prostitute but to remain the faithful bride, trusting God even when life gets really difficult. In 19:10, John is told that it is "the Spirit of prophecy who bears testimony to Jesus." God the Spirit is the source of this prophetic message about Jesus and from Jesus. (Here we see the Spirit's shyness once again.) The Spirit inspires speech about Jesus, words that tell about and glorify Jesus. Not only has the Spirit given John the pictures of what God is up to, but the Spirit has also given John the words to explain how God's plans center on Jesus.

Do you remember a time when God seemed to speak to you very clearly, like a strong sense of direction or an unusual urging? Honestly, it's hard to tell sometimes if you are hearing the voice of God or another voice. But occasionally it is crystal clear. Several years ago I was dealing with a mysterious illness and undergoing all sorts of medical tests. When I hit rock bottom in that long process, I remember crying out to God and the Spirit leading me to read Psalm 103. As I read and thought about the first five verses of that psalm, I felt God speak to me clearly and directly. The Spirit was speaking through God's Word and bringing wisdom and perspective and comfort to a very troubled mind.

Along with giving visions to John and inspiring prophecy, the Spirit also speaks to the seven churches and, by application, to every church in every age. Again, our job is to listen to the voice of the Spirit through his Word. What you notice first is that while Jesus is actually the one speaking to these churches, we are told at the end of each message to listen to what the Spirit is saying (Rev 2:7, 11, 17, 29; 3:6, 13, 22). From this we know that what Jesus says, the Spirit says. Their words are never in conflict in any way. Also, the Spirit continues to speak as the words of Jesus in the book of Revelation are read to churches. Physical hearing is one thing, but spiritual listening takes it to a whole new level. Truly hearing God means that we get serious about doing what he says (see Jesus's parable in Matt 13:1–23). What specifically is the Spirit saying in Revelation 2–3?

The Spirit both comforts the afflicted and afflicts the comfortable, as an old preacher once said. I find myself needing God's comfort one minute and exhortation the next. If you've ever been a camp counselor or worked with kids or been a parent, you know how this works. Kids need to be disciplined and corrected one minute, and the next they need to be consoled and encouraged. We often waver between the extremes of needing a figurative kick in the pants one minute and a literal hug the next. So did the churches of Asia Minor. As we look briefly at what the Spirit is saying to these churches, remember that the Spirit is saying the same thing to us.

The Spirit speaks words of warning and rebuke to these churches. He faults one church for forsaking the love they had when they first became Christians. Several churches are chasing false teaching and the immorality and idolatry it promotes. One church has maintained a solid reputation in their city, but Jesus says they are spiritually dead. A different church is guilty of spiritual self-sufficiency and compromise. They don't think they really need God. Overall, Jesus is very concerned that many of these Christians have become far too comfortable with their pagan culture, resulting in a failure to uphold and live out God's truth.

But the Spirit also speaks words of comfort and encouragement to these congregations. Some have rejected the false teaching and the ungodliness it endorses. Some have suffered hardship and testing and persecution in staying faithful to Jesus. Others have lived faithfully in very difficult and dark cities. Some have given themselves to serving and loving and doing what God desires, even though they feel weak and powerless in the eyes of the world.

Jesus once said, "Whoever has my commands and keeps them is the one who loves me" (John 14:21). This verse echoes Revelation's message. We have to know what God is saying before we can obey, but we can know what he is saying without obeying, without truly listening. When we really hear what the Spirit is saying, we will take his words to heart and let them affect our decisions. Things will change, like how we spend our time and money, how we relate to people, how we pray, and so on. Most of us don't intentionally plug our ears and refuse to listen to the Spirit; we are simply distracted with other things. What distracting voices are hindering your ability to hear the voice of the Spirit?

God's Protective and Comforting Presence

The Holy Spirit also protects and comforts God's people. The "seal of the living God" plays an important role in this theme as well. In Revelation, John doesn't explicitly say that the Holy Spirit is the seal, but this is the most likely interpretation and this same image is clearly used of the Holy Spirit in other parts of the New Testament (2 Cor 1:21–22; Eph 1:13–14; 4:30). The idea of God sealing his people probably comes from the Old Testament book of Ezekiel, where God commands an angel to mark all true believers to protect them from his coming wrath aimed at the Babylonians (Ezek 9:4, 6). The unfaithful Israelites who have not been marked also suffer God's judgment (Ezek 9:5–10). The question of Rev 6:17 (Who can withstand God's wrath?) is answered in 7:1–4—those who have the seal of the living God. The presence of the Holy Spirit, God's seal, means that you will never suffer God's condemning wrath. We don't have to live in fear that God will change his mind and send us to hell. Why? Because he has put his Holy Spirit within us. In other words, the Judge is on our side. He is for us. He lives within us as our Advocate and Comforter.

Have you ever stopped to ask what exactly is new about us when we become Christians? We still sin. We still live in a broken world. We are still going to die. What is the difference between a Christian and a non-Christian? A few things. We have been forgiven, so our past is taken care of and will not be held against us at the final judgment. Also, we have a home in the new creation, so our future is secure. But what about the present? The real difference now is that we have God's Spirit living within us, and unbelievers do not. As the apostle Paul puts it, our bodies are temples of the Holy Spirit, and as a community we form the temple of God's Spirit (1 Cor 3:16; 6:19; Eph 2:22). God is with us and will never leave us.

It's fascinating that in Revelation having God's seal and bearing God's name are the same thing. Both the seal and the name of Christ and God are placed on the person's forehead (7:3; 9:4; 14:1; 22:4). Both identify the people who belong to God, who are truly part of God's covenant community. Those who are not part of God's community receive the mark of the beast on their forehead (13:16; 14:9; 20:4). The seal of God stands in contrast to the mark of the beast. Both marks indicate ownership since they are placed on a person's forehead and are linked to the names of either God and the Lamb or the beast (see 7:3; 13:16–17). One group is sealed for salvation, the other for condemnation.

These are probably not literal marks but spiritual indicators of a person's ultimate allegiance and loyalty, like the fruit of the Spirit or the works of the flesh (see Gal 5:19–24). I know a lot of genuine believers, and none of them has a mark on his or her forehead. Also, these marks or seals are always deliberately chosen in Revelation. They are never obtained by accident or without our knowledge. You don't need to fear that you will be given the mark of the beast without your knowledge. It doesn't work that way. Again, these contrasting marks are not like bar codes or computer chips; rather, they are spiritual indicators of a person's loyalties and allegiances. Those of us who bear God's seal and name will be welcomed into his eternal home because we're part of his family (14:1–5; 2 Tim 2:19).

God's Spirit protects God's people, not against physical suffering but against spiritual defeat. Throughout Revelation we see believers suffering persecution. In 14:13 the Spirit even pronounces an "Amen," or "Yes," to the blessing being given to those who die as faithful followers of Christ: "Then I heard a voice from heaven say, 'Write this: Blessed are the dead who die in the Lord from now on.' 'Yes,' says the Spirit, 'they will rest from their labor, for their deeds will follow them.'"

Not long ago I finished Eric Metaxas's magnificent biography of Dietrich Bonhoeffer, the German pastor and scholar who was executed by the Nazis in the Flossenbürg concentration camp in April 1945. The day before Bonhoeffer was transferred to the camp where he would be martyred, he led his fellow prisoners in a worship service. At its conclusion the guards interrupted the service to take him away, and he knew what that meant. He consoled his friends with these words: "This is the end," he said. "For me the beginning of life." The camp doctor at Flossenbürg gave the following account of Bonhoeffer's last few minutes of life:

> On the morning of that day between five and six o'clock the prisoners, among them Admiral Canaris, General Oster, General Thomas and *Reichgeritsrat* Sack were taken from their cells, and the verdicts of the court martial read out to them. Through the half-open door in one room of the huts I saw Pastor Bonhoeffer, before taking off his prison garb, kneeling on the floor praying fervently to his God. I was most deeply moved by the way this lovable man prayed, so devout and so certain that God heard his prayer. At the place of execution, he again said a short prayer and then climbed the steps to the gallows, brave and composed. His death ensued after a few seconds. In the almost fifty years that I worked as a doctor, I have hardly ever seen a man die so entirely submissive to the will of God.[3]

Having the seal of God's Spirit does not exempt us from physical suffering, but the Spirit does guarantee spiritual protection and empowerment against Satan and his demonic forces or their human pawns (9:4). The seal of God's Spirit will enable us to remain faithful to Christ and not renounce him when we are pressured to do so by hostile powers.

The Holy Spirit in the Heavenly City

If you've ever worked with kids, you know they can ask the toughest theological questions. It's not hard to imagine a five-year-old asking, "Hey, Mom, where does God live?" Revelation helps us answer that particular question in a pretty cool way, although it may take a few paragraphs to spell out the answer.

In the Old Testament story of the exodus, we read about God's glorious presence among the people: "By day the LORD went ahead of them in a pillar of cloud to guide them on their way and by night in a pillar of fire to give them light, so that they could travel by day or night" (Exod 13:21). In time, the Lord instructed them to make a portable place for him to live among the people: "Then have them make a sanctuary [tabernacle] for me, and I will dwell among them" (25:8). God lived among the people in a tabernacle, or tent, during their wilderness journey. God's presence filled the tabernacle: "Then the cloud covered the tent of meeting, and the glory of the Lord filled the tabernacle" (40:34). God's "Shekinah" (from the Hebrew verb *shakan*, meaning "to dwell," the same verb from which *mishkan*, "tabernacle," is derived) refers to his glorious and radiant dwelling or presence among his people. The divine presence in the tabernacle traveled with the people throughout their wilderness wanderings and during their conquest of the promised land. The Jerusalem temple finally took the place of the tabernacle as the dwelling place for God's presence.

Now perhaps you can see why John 1:14 is so shockingly wonderful: "The Word [Jesus Christ] became flesh and made his dwelling [literally, "pitched his tent," or "tabernacled"] among us. We have seen his glory, the glory of the one and only Son, who came from the Father, full of grace and truth." Notice the connection between dwelling and glory. Those who walked with Jesus actually experienced the glorious presence of God, the Shekinah.

What about us? How do we experience God's glorious presence? We are told in Rev 21:3 that eventually God will bring us into the new heaven and new earth and live among us: "And I heard a loud voice from the throne saying, 'Look! God's dwelling place [the noun "tabernacle"] is now among the people, and he will dwell [the verb "tabernacle"] with them. They will be his people, and God himself will be with them and be their God.'" Also in 7:15 we learn that God will cover or shelter his people with his presence in heaven: "Therefore, 'they are before the throne of God and serve him day and night in his temple; and he who sits on the throne will shelter [or "tabernacle"] them with his presence.'"

79

So, in the new creation, God's presence will cover and shelter us. Interestingly, we are told that we will experience God's sheltering presence "before his throne" (1:4). We saw earlier that God's Spirit (referred to as the "seven spirits") takes his place before the throne (1:4; 4:5). The expression "before his throne" indicates the presence of God. This same idea is stated negatively when we read in chapter 13 that the beast blasphemes God and slanders his name "and his dwelling place, that is, those who live in heaven" (13:6, my translation; cf. 12:12). Our eternal home is in God's Shekinah, his glorious presence. That's one reason the new Jerusalem takes the shape of a cube, the same shape as the Most Holy Place, or, holy of holies in the ancient temple (21:16). We will spend eternity in God's presence, with nothing to fear and everything to enjoy.

To connect the dots: the Spirit who will shelter and cover us in the new creation before God's throne is the same Spirit who lives within and among us now on earth. God's sheltering, protecting, comforting presence covers us when we become followers of Jesus. God has now come to us by his Spirit, the Spirit who is God's "before-the-throne" Shekinah presence. Wow! We experience God's heavenly presence now through our relationship to the Holy Spirit, both in our individual bodies and in our community of believers.

Do you sense that you are experiencing God's glorious presence? If not, perhaps it's time to confess your sins, especially the sins of the body, the Spirit's temple. Perhaps it's time for a deep, confessional detox as you have an honest conversation with God. Paul's words in 1 Cor 6:18–20 seem appropriate here:

> Flee from sexual immorality. All other sins a person commits are outside the body, but whoever sins sexually, sins against their own body. Do you not know that your bodies are temples of the Holy Spirit, who is in you, whom you have received from God?

You are not your own; you were bought at a price. Therefore
honor God with your bodies.

If sexual sins are entrenched in your life, you might need to talk
with someone and get help breaking this addiction.

Since the church is also the body of Christ, you may need
to confess any sins against your community. I read a tweet
recently that went something like, "The deeper we are with
Jesus, the more we will forgive our enemies." God takes it
very, very seriously when his children don't get along, because
unity is a big deal to God and is one of the main ways that
we tell a hurting world that a relationship with Jesus makes
life much better (see John 17 and Ephesians 4 for more on the
importance of unity).

In the final chapters of Revelation, there are other images
we read about that point to the Spirit:

- There will be no temple in the heavenly city since God and
  the Lamb will be the temple (21:22). In other words, we
  will live in the place where God's Spirit lives permanently.
- The heavenly city will not have a sun or moon, for the
  glory of the Lord God will give it light (21:23–25; 22:5).
  As we saw from 4:5, the seven lamps (the seven spirits of
  God, or the Holy Spirit) supply heavenly light.
- Jesus told people to follow him in order to find rivers of
  living water, which he identified as the Holy Spirit (see
  John 4:4–26; 7:37–39). In the heavenly city, we will drink
  of this living water (Rev 7:14–17; 21:6; 22:1–2, 17).

In the heavenly city, the Spirit will make known important
realities, such as light and living water. These are things we
crave now. We want light and no more darkness, no more
suffering, no more death. We want living water, which means
healing and provision and abundance. We want life rather than

death. When we turn to Jesus, the Holy Spirit comes to live within us. By giving us his Spirit, God is saying to us: "Here is life and healing and provision now and the promise of ultimate life to come."

Conclusion

I grew up in a tradition that didn't pay a lot of attention to the Holy Spirit. In fact, I've had to work most of my life to stop calling the Spirit an "it" and refer to the Spirit instead as the Third Person of the Trinity that he is. If it helps, there are times in the Bible when the Holy Spirit is called the Spirit of God (e.g., Matt 3:16; 12:28) or the Spirit of Christ (Rom 8:9; Phil 1:19; 1 Pet 1:11). The bottom line is that we experience God through the Holy Spirit. God lives within us as believers and works in this world by his Spirit. If we neglect the Spirit, we neglect God. You can't be "spiritual" without the Spirit because "Spiritual" includes anything that lines up with and is blessed by the Holy Spirit.

We've seen that in the book of Revelation the Holy Spirit is alive and well. God isn't just resting on his throne while important things need to be done in this world. He is working mightily in this world by his Spirit. As we pay attention to the role of the Spirit, we will grasp more fully the message of Revelation. We will understand how God lives within and among us rather than looking for God's presence in a religious experience or charismatic personality. We will gain perspective about how God works in this world rather than relying on the might of human creativity. God works mightily through his Spirit, who often shines brilliantly through the dullness of human weakness. We will be able to hear the voice of God by listening carefully to the Spirit-inspired Word of God. And as we trust in the protective and comforting presence of the Spirit, we won't be driven and tossed around by all sorts of fears. Finally, we can look forward to the Spirit's role in the future heavenly city. That's important because we begin to experience now in the Spirit some of what we will experience fully in the new heaven and new earth. The Spirit brings a hopeful preview of what God has in store for us one day.

Key texts: Rev 1:4; 4:5; 5:6; 14:13–14; 19:10
Reading plan: Revelation 7

Community Group Questions

1. What is your religious background when it comes to the Holy Spirit? On a spectrum between total neglect and total fixation, where would you fall? How does your background influence your views of the Spirit now?

2. God works in this world by his Spirit. When do you find yourself trying to "do the Christian life" apart from the wisdom and strength and power provided by the Spirit? What tricks us into thinking that we can live this life apart from God's Spirit?

3. What helps you hear the voice of the Spirit as you read and study the Bible? What are your greatest challenges in this area?

4. How does knowing you have been sealed with the Spirit of God encourage you to live boldly and courageously?

5. Can you tell about a time when the Spirit provided comfort for you?

6. What kinds of things keep Christians today from experiencing God's glorious presence? How can your community help people break free of these things?

7. We talked about some of the things the Spirit will do in the new creation, and we said that we often begin to experience some of those realities now. Would you say that you've already started to see some of those things happen in your life? In what way?

5

OUR ENEMIES

"The Dragon Stood on the Shore of the Sea"

Whether we like it or not, we are involved in a spiritual battle (Eph 6:10–20). God's enemies are our enemies. Revelation speaks of supernatural and human enemies, such as the devil, demons, the Antichrist, the false prophet, wicked humans, and evil empires, which mount a relentless attack on believers. And because these forces of evil have already lost the war for ultimate control of the universe, they fight the smaller battles viciously, like cornered, wounded animals (12:12). There is no neutrality in this cosmic conflict. You have to choose sides. And while there may be occasional cease-fires or lapses in the fighting, we will always be in a spiritual struggle this side of the new creation. It's fair to say that we live in a war zone.

Revelation reveals the various strategies and tactics of our enemies, chiefly accusation, deception, temptation, and persecution. The book reassures us that God has already won the major battle of the war at the cross and resurrection of Jesus

Christ. Armageddon may lie in the future, but it's only the
devil's last act of defiance rather than a battle to determine the
outcome of history. Although the war has been won, there are
still plenty of battles remaining, and Revelation explains how
we are supposed to fight these battles. We win not by trusting
in human weaponry, whether it be military, economic, political,
or religious, but by relying on what Christ has done and by
obeying the Lord even when it costs us, trusting that God will
vindicate his people in the end (12:11). In other words, we
fight by following Jesus faithfully and testifying to God's truth.

Earth Dwellers and Empires

Growing up as a Christian in the Bible Belt of America, I came
up with a really strange notion that when people walk with
the Lord, everyone will respect them and think well of them.
In other words, committed Christians should have no human
enemies, only friends. This wasn't a belief I got from studying
the Bible; it was an idea absorbed from my culture. While there
is some truth to righteous living producing a good reputation,
it's a bit naive and just plain wrong to think that as dedicated
Christians we will never have human enemies. We will. Jesus
had enemies and told us we would too, and he taught us how
to respond to them. In Revelation, we see plenty of examples
of believers facing human opposition.

In the messages to the seven churches, we meet groups of false
teachers who pretend to be extra-spiritual Christians with the
freedom to do just about anything (2:2). Revelation mentions
the Nicolaitans (2:6, 15), those who hold to the teachings of
Balaam (2:14), and Jezebel and her followers (2:20–23). The
term "Nicolaitans" means "victorious over the people" or "victory people" and probably reflects a wordplay on the important
word *nikaō* ("overcome" or "be victorious") used throughout
the book (2:7, 11, 17, 26; 3:5, 12, 21; 5:5; 6:2; 11:7; 12:11;
13:7; 15:2; 17:14; 21:7). These different groups likely had a

similar belief system: Christians can participate in the paganism of the culture (e.g., sexual immorality and worship of false
gods) and still be faithful Christians. In contrast, Jesus teaches
that we can't give our bodies to sinful habits and expect God's
approval for doing so (read 2:16, 20–25). What we do with
our bodies matters and actually reflects our true spirituality.

Believers in the seven churches also faced opposition from
some of the Jews in their communities. The Jews were exempted
from worshiping the Roman emperor because Judaism was
tolerated as an ancient monotheistic religion. Throughout most
of the first century, Christians and Jews were closely identified,
resulting in some protection for Christians. But with the persecutions under Emperor Nero in the mid 60s, the authorities
began to view Christianity as a new religion not to be tolerated.
As a result, some Jews uttered "slander" (*blasphēmia* in 2:9)
against Christians or accused them before the Roman authorities, resulting in persecution. Perhaps the Jews did this because
they rejected Jesus as the Messiah or because too many of their
friends were converting to Christianity or because they felt the
Christians were misinterpreting the Jewish law. Who knows? In
any case, Jesus says the Jews who were persecuting his disciples
are not true Jews at all. They are, in reality, a "synagogue of
Satan" rather than a congregation of God's true people (2:9).
To another church Jesus says, "I will make those who are of
the synagogue of Satan, who claim to be Jews though they are
not, but are liars—I will make them come and fall down at your
feet and acknowledge that I have loved you" (3:9).

The Jewish condemnation of Christians continued into the
second century, when the Jews betrayed Polycarp, a disciple of
the apostle John and bishop of Smyrna, resulting in his martyrdom. The account of his death is the oldest written account
of a Christian martyr outside the New Testament:

> As Polycarp was being taken into the arena, a voice came to him
> from heaven: "Be strong, Polycarp and play the man!" No one

saw who had spoken, but our brothers who were there heard the voice. When the crowd heard that Polycarp had been captured, there was an uproar. The Proconsul asked him whether he was Polycarp. On hearing that he was, he tried to persuade him to apostatize, saying, "Have respect for your old age, swear by the fortune of Caesar. Repent, and say, 'Down with the Atheists!'" Polycarp looked grimly at the wicked heathen multitude in the stadium, and gesturing towards them, he said, "Down with the Atheists!" "Swear," urged the Proconsul, "reproach Christ, and I will set you free." "86 years have I served him," Polycarp declared, "and he has done me no wrong. How can I blaspheme my King and my Savior?"[1]

Notice that both of these groups who opposed the church (the false teachers and the false Jews) were very religious. They differ among themselves as to their views on morality and their relationship to the prevailing culture, but both the false teachers and the false Jews are religious. It's easy for people to feel as if God is always on their side, even when he hates what they are doing. Don't be surprised if at some point in your life you face opposition from people who claim to be true believers. Revelation reminds us that not all religion is from God and that not everyone who claims to speak for God actually does. When opposed by religious enemies, we need the humility to return again to the teachings of Christ and we need the wisdom and courage to respond in a way that pleases him.

Revelation also teaches that human opposition will come from unbelievers. The expression "inhabitants of the earth," or "earth dwellers," occurs ten times in Revelation (3:10; 6:10; 8:13; 11:10; 13:8, 12, 14 [2x]; 17:2, 8) and always refers to unbelievers, meaning people who are in direct rebellion against God. They worship the beast and commit adultery with the great prostitute (13:8, 12, 14; 17:2, 8). They mock and persecute God's people (6:10; 11:10). As a result, their names are not written in the book of life, and they will suffer God's wrath (3:10; 8:13; 17:8). The Bible makes it clear that those who follow Christ can expect to encounter the hatred and antagonism of those who don't. For example, Jesus says, "Blessed are you when people insult you, persecute you and falsely say all kinds of evil against you because of me" (Matt 5:11), and the apostle Paul warns, "Everyone who wants to live a godly life in Christ Jesus will be persecuted" (2 Tim 3:12).

This doesn't mean, of course, that all non-Christians hate Christians. But it does mean that Christians shouldn't be surprised by opposition in this world. We shouldn't seek it, but we shouldn't be shocked when it happens. Christians in America are generally ignorant of how fellow believers are being persecuted around the world today. At a recent conference in Rome entitled "International Religious Liberty and the Global Clash of Values," Pope Francis said he was "greatly pained to note that Christians around the world are suffering the greatest part of this discrimination. The persecution of Christians today is even greater than in the first centuries of the Church, and there are more Christian martyrs today than in that era."[2] Evangelical scholars and organizations that keep track of such suffering tend to agree.[3]

Revelation also speaks of wicked empires that oppose God and his people. The great center of pagan power in Revelation is called "Babylon the Great" or "the great prostitute." In the first century, no doubt, the Roman Empire was in view, but there have been anti-Christian empires in almost every age. In chapters 17–19, John writes in detail about the character and actions of Babylon, the wicked empire of the first century. God condemns this great prostitute for four specific sins: (1) she glorifies herself and rejects God through arrogant self-sufficiency and idolatry; (2) she promotes sexual immorality; (3) she indulges in excessive luxury and materialism to the neglect of human need; and (4) she abuses and murders those who follow Jesus Christ.[4] Any society or aspect of a society, be it religious or not, that reproduces these traits could rightly be called part of Babylon.

89

You've probably heard the story about the frog in boiling water. If you put a frog in boiling water, it will immediately jump out. But if you put the frog in cold water and slowly heat the water, it won't jump out but will just sit there and boil to death. The story illustrates the truth that people don't often react to important changes that occur gradually. Ungodly empires are intoxicating. Their pleasures and benefits cast a spell over us, and before we know it, they dominate us in a thousand ways. We have to ask ourselves how much we are captivated by the empire(s) we encounter. How addicted are we to the sports or entertainment industry? Have we become desensitized to sin in the media? (Do we sometimes use humor to condone or excuse empire immorality that the Bible explicitly condemns?) Are we pursuing wealth for selfish purposes, or do we give generously and sacrificially?

The truth is that God takes sin far more seriously than we do. According to Revelation, God's judgment of Babylon will be devastating and is 100 percent certain to happen: "Therefore in one day her plagues will overtake her: death, mourning and famine. She will be consumed by fire, for mighty is the Lord God who judges her" (18:8). That's why God tells his church plainly, "'Come out of her, my people,' so that you will not share in her sins, so that you will not receive any of her plagues" (18:4).

The Unholy Trinity

Human enemies and worldly empires are empowered and motivated and enslaved by the more permanent and powerful demonic empire of Satan. As the apostle Paul puts it, "Our struggle is not against flesh and blood, but against the rulers, against the authorities, against the powers of this dark world and against the spiritual forces of evil in the heavenly realms" (Eph 6:12). Just as there is the Holy Trinity of Father, Son, and Spirit, so Revelation describes an unholy trinity of the dragon (Satan) and the two beasts.

The red dragon, or Satan, is the archenemy of God and his people. In Revelation 2–3 we've already seen how Satan stands behind the persecution of God's people, but we don't get the full picture until chapter 12, where we read of a great red dragon (Satan) waiting to devour the male child (Jesus). After failing to kill the child, he attacks the woman and her offspring (God's people). He can't get to them either because he and his demonic angels have already lost the war in heaven against Michael and his angels, a war that probably reflects his defeat at the cross and resurrection of Jesus on earth. At the last judgment, Satan and his demonic forces will be condemned to eternal torment (20:7–10; Matt 25:41). But in the meantime, he does a lot of damage and constitutes the ultimate source of the persecution of the saints.

The devil cannot overpower God's people spiritually and steal them from God since the Holy Spirit has sealed us with his protective presence. As a result, he must try to deceive or accuse or persecute believers. The term "devil" means "accuser" or "slanderer" and reflects his main strategy: to accuse us before God (12:10) and try to deceive us so that we turn from God (12:9). Deception and accusation are both based in lies. For Satan to have any power over us, we have to move away from God's truth and, at least for a short time, believe a lie. Consequently, we need to know God's truth, which is communicated to us through his Word. Taking refuge in God's truth includes knowing God's story in the Bible, knowing how to interpret and apply sections of the Bible, being part of a community where God's Word is honored and taught well, and consistently memorizing and meditating on and praying the Scriptures.

I've never been scuba diving, but I'm told that it's a blast.[5] Strapping on those life tanks and exploring the water world below sounds like fun. Of course, it's not all fun and games. A former Navy diver once was telling me that he had been in waters so deep and dark that it was almost impossible to keep from becoming disoriented and confused. I thought, *What a terrifying feeling it must be—underwater, unable to see your hands in front of your face, not knowing which way is up, panic engulfing you.* I immediately interrupted my friend. "So, what do you do when that happens?" I knew he had survived such ordeals since he was standing there talking to me. "Feel the bubbles," he said. "When it's pitch-black and you have no idea which way to go, you reach up with your hand and feel the bubbles. The bubbles always drift to the surface. When you can't trust your feelings or judgment, you can always trust the bubbles to get you back to the top." Life is like scuba diving in that we need a way to determine what is real and true when we can't trust our feelings or intuition. The Bible is our reality book, an amazing gift from God to help know what is true and real, to help us avoid the devil's deceptive schemes.

So Satan is a defeated but still dangerous enemy who needs to be resisted (Jas 4:7; 1 Pet 5:9). I'm convinced that one of the chief ways Satan tries to deceive Christians today is through distractions. We simply lose sight of what is important and what we're supposed to be doing. We get disoriented and sidetracked and find ourselves drifting and spending our life on stupid stuff that doesn't matter. We're overstimulated by social media and distracted to death. When we give in to these little distractions over time, they can lead to big tragedies in our lives. We become deceived and led astray. This is how Satan works. Although it's important to say no to distractions, perhaps we need to focus more on saying yes to the few things we know God wants us to do. Distractions melt away when we pursue the Lord and his calling on our lives with a sense of urgency.

Revelation 12:11 sums up the whole book in one verse: "They [Christians] triumphed over him [Satan] by the blood of the Lamb and by the word of their testimony; they did not love their lives so much as to shrink from death." This verse tells us how Christians conquer the devil. First, we rely on the finished work of Christ, who shed his blood on the cross for our sins.

Satan's accusations against us don't hold water, because we're relying not on our own works but on the completed work of Christ on the cross. Second, we continue to trust Christ and his faithfulness ("the word of their testimony") no matter what. We focus on saying yes to Jesus and what he has done for us. This becomes our consuming passion in life. We will not be deceived when we fix our eyes on Jesus.

As Revelation 13 opens, we see the dragon taking his stand on the shore of the sea (a common symbol of evil in the Bible), and from the sea he calls forth a beast. There are actually two beasts in Revelation: the beast from the sea (traditionally called the Antichrist) and the beast from the earth (traditionally dubbed the false prophet). It's important to realize that Satan doesn't try to fight every battle himself. He is God's opponent but not God's opposite, meaning he is not all-powerful or everywhere present or all-knowing. Satan works mostly through ungodly systems and leaders to wage his war against God and his followers.

Revelation 13 tells us more about the two beasts who partner with Satan. The beasts represent wicked empires empowered by Satan. Individual evil leaders, like Nero or Domitian in the first century or Adolf Hitler in the twentieth century, often personify and put a face on these evil systems. This explains how both beasts can seem like a person and yet appear much larger and more powerful than an individual. The first beast represents political, military, and economic power used in the service of Satan, while the second beast represents false religious power that serves as a propaganda machine for the first beast. While the first beast is often referred to as the "Antichrist," that term is never actually used in Revelation. Also, the mark of the beast, or 666, refers to a Roman emperor, like Nero.[6] The first Christians almost certainly identified the first beast as the Roman Empire and its emperor.

The second beast is called the false prophet and probably refers to the imperial cult, a religious system that promoted the worship of the emperor and other pagan gods. I think it's appropriate to know how the first Christians interpreted these images, although the images probably also apply to evil empires and their leaders and "religions" of every age. John writes in 1 John 2:18: "Dear children, this is the last hour; and as you have heard that the antichrist is coming, even now many antichrists have come." Any power system that opposes the triune God and demands absolute allegiance or worship would fit the description.

The two beasts function as Satan's puppets. They tell lies against believers (13:6), subject them to economic persecution (13:16–17), try to deceive them with miraculous signs (13:13–15), and punish them if they remain loyal to God rather than to the secular system (13:7, 10, 15). They will face Christ's judgment at his return (17:8; 19:19–21), but until then, they must be resisted.

Together the dragon and the two beasts form the unholy trinity. There is nothing good in them, but they try their best to imitate good. One reason we should reject evil is that it's a third-rate copy or fake imitation of what God has done. God raised Jesus from the dead, while the beast is said to have been healed from a death wound (13:3, 14).[7] God has sealed or protected his people, while the beast offers a mark for his followers (13:16–17). God has his throne in heaven, while the beast also has his throne (13:2). The beast also demands worship as a parody of the worship of God (13:8, 14–15).

Since evil has no energy or life within itself, it must always imitate good to gain any traction at all. Cornelius Plantinga writes:

> Satan must appeal to our God-given appetite for goodness in order to win his way. . . . To prevail, evil must leech not only power and intelligence from goodness but also its credibility. From counterfeit money to phony airliner parts to the

trustworthy look on the face of a con artist, evil appears in disguise. Hence its treacherousness.[8]

This explains why it's incredibly important for us to know what is real and true and to use wisdom and discernment as we seek to stay faithful (see 13:9–10, 18). The mature believer will learn to discern the Spirit's true voice when trying to distinguish good from evil.

God's Ultimate Victory

I've had the privilege of leading several study trips to Israel. Usually on our first full day of touring, we visit the ancient city of Megiddo and nearby Mount Carmel. The famous "Armageddon" of Revelation means "mountain of Megiddo." But since there is no mountain of Megiddo, the connection seems to be more general and symbolic. The surrounding valley, which you can see from the top of Mount Carmel, was the site of many ancient battles where God's people were attacked by pagan nations. It seems appropriate that Armageddon represents an epic, end-time battle between God and the forces of evil.

Armageddon is mentioned only in Revelation 16, but the battle itself is described in chapter 19. In 16:13–14 we read that the counterfeit trinity speaks forth demonic spirits to gather the wicked for "the battle on the great day of God Almighty." Evil uses demon-inspired rhetoric and propaganda to deceive many into opposing God.

Before we look at Revelation 19 and the actual battle, we need to pay close attention to the parenthesis in 16:15, where Jesus says, "Look, I come like a thief! Blessed is the one who stays awake and remains clothed, so as not to go naked and be shamefully exposed." This is a good example of why there is so much confusion about Revelation. Almost everyone has heard about Armageddon, but few have heard about Jesus's beatitude in this verse. Yet, 16:15 provides the central message for us in light of the coming battle. Heeding Jesus's words here is much more important than figuring out Armageddon. Jesus had already warned his followers to stay alert since his return would occur suddenly, like a thief coming in the middle of the night (e.g., Matt 24:43; Luke 12:39). Nakedness symbolizes shame, guilt, and liability to judgment (Rev 3:3–5, 17–18). Jesus is telling us that Babylon can lull us to sleep spiritually. Rather than giving all our energy to speculating about the end-time battle and when and where it might occur, we need to be faithful in fighting the personal battles that come our way every day. This is what it means to stay awake and alert. To remain watchful means to remain faithful to Jesus. Simple obedience may not be as exciting as solving an apocalyptic puzzle, but it's much more important.

Well, I hate to disappoint you, but the actual battle of Armageddon is really a nonbattle. It begins with the return of Christ. While Jesus came to earth the first time as a helpless baby for the purpose of entering into our human condition and ultimately dying on the cross for our sins, he returns as the Warrior Messiah for the purpose of destroying evil once and for all. The description of the battle-ready Jesus in 19:11–16 sounds fearsome indeed. Then we read about the battle of Armageddon in 19:19–21:

> Then I saw the beast and the kings of the earth and their armies gathered together to wage war against the rider on the horse and his army. But the beast was captured, and with it the false prophet. . . . The two of them were thrown alive into the fiery lake of burning sulfur. The rest were killed with the sword coming out of the mouth of the rider on the horse, and all the birds gorged themselves on their flesh.

Sorry—I told you it would be anticlimactic: "But the beast was captured." That's it. Jesus wins simply by appearing. The

King of kings and Lord of lords conquers and judges evil by his word (the sword of his mouth in v. 15). This takes care of the two beasts, but what about the dragon?

Revelation 20 and the whole Millennium issue can get quite complicated.[9] The gist of it is that for a time the dragon will be imprisoned. Following his release, he will lead the wicked in one final act of rebellion and attempt to destroy God's people (no surprise there). At this point, God has had enough and throws Satan into the fiery lake, where he will be tormented forever. The wicked then face God's judgment (see 20:11–15). In the end, Satan and his army of demons, the two beasts, and all wicked humans, as well as death itself, have been cast into the lake of fire, a symbol of final judgment.

When Revelation 21 opens, all evil has been eliminated, and God is making everything new—a new heaven and new earth, a new heavenly city, and believers with new bodies—and God will live among his people forever. In addition, there will be no more sin, evil, enemies, crying, mourning, pain, or death. "It is done," God says. "I am the Alpha and the Omega, the Beginning and the End. . . . Those who are victorious will inherit all this, and I will be their God and they will be my children" (21:6–7).

How We Fight

One thing is clear from Revelation: God and his people are at war with the forces of evil. The outcome of this war is certain. We don't have to wait for Armageddon, as New Testament scholar Grant Osborne reminds us:

> He [Satan] has already lost, for the great victory in the Apocalypse occurs not at Armageddon but at the cross. It was the slain Lamb who achieved the great victory (5:6, 12), and the devil "knows his time is short" (12:12). Armageddon is not the final battle but the last act of defiance by an already defeated foe.[10]

God has already won the cosmic war, even though there are still many important battles remaining. I don't know all that will happen to me or my family or my friends, but I know that ultimately we win.

Over and over again in Revelation we are told to "overcome," or "conquer" (Gk. *nikaō*). In Revelation 2–3 promises are made to those who overcome. Then at the end of the book we see the fulfillment of those promises as the victors inherit God's eternal kingdom and live forever in his presence (e.g., 21:7). But what exactly does it mean to overcome or conquer? How are we supposed to fight the battles that remain? How do we win the victory?

Revelation has seven beatitudes (or "blessings"), and they tell us a lot about what it means to overcome or conquer:[11]

- "**Blessed** is the one who reads aloud the words of this prophecy, and **blessed** are those who hear it and take to heart what is written in it, because the time is near" (1:3).

- "Then I heard a voice from heaven say, 'Write this: **Blessed** are the dead who die in the Lord from now on.' 'Yes,' says the Spirit, 'they will rest from their labor, for their deeds will follow them'" (14:13).

- "Look, I come like a thief! **Blessed** is the one who stays awake and remains clothed, so as not to go naked and be shamefully exposed" (16:15).

- "Then the angel said to me, 'Write this: **Blessed** are those who are invited to the wedding supper of the Lamb!' And he added, 'These are the true words of God'" (19:9).

- "**Blessed** and holy are those who share in the first resurrection. The second death has no power over them, but they will be priests of God and of Christ and will reign with him for a thousand years" (20:6).

- "Look, I am coming soon! **Blessed** is the one who keeps the words of the prophecy written in this scroll" (22:7).
- "**Blessed** are those who wash their robes, that they may have the right to the tree of life and may go through the gates into the city. Outside are the dogs, those who practice magic arts, the sexually immoral, the murderers, the idolaters and everyone who loves and practices false-hood" (22:14–15).

These blessings show us that those who overcome (1) hear and obey God's Word, (2) turn away from sin, and (3) persevere in following the Lamb until the end. To put it bluntly, overcoming means we say no to sin and yes to God, and we continue doing that until the end. We say no to false teaching and sexual immorality and idolatry and compromise. We say yes to trust and service and endurance and suffering. When we falter or stray, we repent and return to the Lamb, whose sacrifice makes our forgiveness possible. We could sum it up this way: to overcome means we follow the Lamb with our whole life to the very end of our life.

One very ironic thing about overcoming is this—we overcome by being overcome. We read in 11:7 that the beast attacks the two witnesses and "overpowers," or conquers, them. Later we read that the beast was given power to make war against the saints and "conquer" them (13:7). Throughout history the forces of evil have "conquered" God's people by inflicting on them physical persecution and death. But that's not the end of the story. We learn from 12:11 that believers "triumphed over [or "overcame"] him by the blood of the Lamb and by the word of their testimony; they did not love their lives so much as to shrink from death." Jesus overcame by dying on the cross and being raised from the dead. Satan's "victory" over him in death was in reality Jesus's victory over Satan.

To overcome by being overcome means that we stay faithful even if it means persecution or martyrdom, because God has already conquered death through Jesus's resurrection, which in turn guarantees our resurrection and victory. At the end of C. S. Lewis's *The Lion, the Witch and the Wardrobe*, the children run to the broken stone table expecting to find a dead Aslan but are amazed to meet the very-much-alive Aslan instead. After they are convinced that he is real and not a ghost, Susan asks what it all means, and Aslan provides the answer:

> "It means," said Aslan, "that though the Witch knew the Deep Magic, there is a magic deeper still which she did not know. Her knowledge goes back only to the dawn of Time. But if she could have looked a little further back, into the stillness and the darkness before Time dawned, she would have read there a different incantation. She would have known that when a willing victim who had committed no treachery was killed in a traitor's stead, the Table would crack and Death itself would start working backwards."[12]

The answer is that victory comes through sacrifice. We also follow Christ's pattern. Yes, the cross of Christ was unique, since only Jesus could suffer as the perfect sacrifice for our sins. But he also calls us to deny ourselves, *take up our cross*, and follow him (see Mark 8:34–35). We overcome by being faithful even in the midst of suffering, even if it costs us our physical life. Our names have been written in the Lamb's book of life, so even if they take our lives, we still have life. Our God is the God of resurrection life!

One last thing about how we fight, but it's a really important thing to know: Several times in Revelation God's people are described as an army of followers (e.g., 7:1–8; 17:14; 19:14, 19). But what is most interesting is these warriors don't really fight. We participate in Christ's victory primarily by following our Lord. We fight by following. Our only weapon is to give a faithful witness to God's truth in Jesus Christ. As it says in 14:4, "They follow the Lamb wherever he goes." That's what it means to be a disciple of Jesus.

Conclusion

To say that we conquer by being conquered is one thing, but to live this way is an entirely different matter. Almost everything in our culture is contrary to this notion. In business or sports or school or even church, the name of the game is to win, to conquer, to be victorious. Competition is a dominant code of our culture. Almost every aspect of life calls us to try to win something or to beat somebody.

Let's clarify a moment. Revelation isn't suggesting that we have to stop trying to win the flag football game or that losing at spades is more spiritual than winning or that we can't be a fan of any sports team. Sometimes a bit of friendly competition is nothing more than harmless fun. (A side note: in any situation it helps my mind-set to focus more on striving for excellence than on defeating the other guy.) The problem is that we sometimes carry this idea of winning over into the Christian faith, where we begin to assume that being a Christian means no suffering, no trials, no sacrifice, no persecution. We think that kind of stuff can't happen to us because we're followers of Jesus and we always win. But the truth of the matter is that we follow the one who suffered and died on a cross. Let that sink in. In the world's eyes, we're already losers. Ultimately we have to trust that God's resurrection power will overcome any temporary defeat we experience now. We follow the risen Christ! Our victory is certain. Even when we "lose," we've already won.

Key texts: Rev 6:10–11; 12:7–9, 13–17; 18:4
Reading plan: Revelation 12–13; 17–18; 20

Community Group Questions

1. What is the first thing that comes to mind when you think about spiritual warfare? How does the book of Revelation change your beliefs about our enemies or about our battles?

2. Did you grow up as I did, with the notion that everyone will respect Christians? In other words, do you expect to face opposition as a normal part of living as a Christian?

3. Jesus was pretty hard on the false teachers in Revelation who felt they could be faithful while compromising with the pagan culture. What is your reaction to his reaction?

4. How informed would you say you are about the persecuted church around the world? Why do you think this is a topic that so many of us don't hear much about? What can we do to support them?

5. Revelation has a lot to say about wicked empires such as Babylon. What do you think makes an empire wicked? (You might want to read portions of Revelation 18.)

6. What have you learned about how Revelation portrays Satan or how we should respond to his deceptive attacks?

7. How does Revelation help you know how to fight spiritual battles wisely and faithfully?

6

THE MISSION

"My Two Witnesses"

I love a good novel. Because Hollywood really can't compete with our God-given imaginations, I usually prefer a good book to a movie (except for the popcorn). As I read, I get into the story and identify with the characters and want things to go a certain way and complain when they don't. Stories are powerful. It's sad to me that there aren't more biblical scholars writing novels. Most attempts to write a novel based on the Bible either ignore the biblical context or butcher it. Things tend to get worse when such novels focus on apocalyptic themes.

There are a few delightful exceptions to the common disconnect between biblical scholars and novels. One is the book by Bruce Longenecker entitled *The Lost Letters of Pergamum*.[1] His story is set in the first century and features a character who also appears in Revelation: Antipas. As the story goes, Antipas, a Roman civic leader, encounters the writings of Luke, the biblical author of both the Gospel of Luke and Acts. Antipas and Luke begin corresponding, and, long story short, Antipas becomes a believer. A gladiatorial contest in Pergamum forces a difficult decision on the local Christians, especially Antipas. I won't spoil the end of the story, but Antipas stands strong as a faithful witness.

In Revelation, there are only a few named characters. Interestingly, two of the named good guys (John and Antipas) are described in similar ways. We are told that John is in exile on the small island of Patmos "because of the word of God and the testimony of Jesus" (1:9). In other words, he's in trouble for being a faithful witness. In the message to the church at Pergamum, Jesus identifies Antipas as "my faithful witness" (2:13). Both John and Antipas are faithful witnesses. It is no coincidence that in the book's opening greeting, Jesus himself is described as "*the* faithful witness" (1:5; cf. 3:14). What an honor for John and Antipas to be put in the same category as Jesus—faithful witnesses![2] In this chapter, we will look closely at our mission as God's people: to be faithful witnesses to Jesus and his kingdom.

God's Love for the Nations

"Red and yellow, black and white, they are precious in his sight; Jesus loves the little children of the world"—so goes the children's song. While many believe that Revelation is about only warfare and judgment, you might be surprised to learn that Revelation also shows God's deep love for the nations, the people being deceived by Satan. While "the inhabitants of the earth" is always a negative description of the wicked in Revelation, the term "nations" can go either way—some oppose the Lord (e.g., 20:8), while others submit to him (e.g., 22:2). God's heart longs for the nations to turn back to him in repentance, and he wills to have a people that will include individuals from "every tribe and language and people and nation" (5:9). As the familiar John 3:16 puts it, "For God so loved the *world* that he gave his one and only Son."

God loves the nations by speaking his message to them. John is told in Rev 10:11 that he "must prophesy again about many peoples, nations, languages and kings." In Revelation

14, another angel goes forth with the eternal gospel, proclaiming "to those who live on the earth—to every nation, tribe, language and people," calling them to "fear God and give him glory" and to "worship him who made the heavens, the earth, the sea and the springs of water" (14:6–7). Again, this group is not identical to the ungodly "inhabitants of the earth," and hope remains that some among the nations might convert, or "fear God and give him glory."

Throughout Revelation the nations are shown to be vulnerable and susceptible to deceptive powers of darkness. In chapter 17, the prostitute sits on many waters, later defined as "peoples, multitudes, nations and languages" (17:15). In chapter 18, the great harlot is said to have led astray or deceived the nations (18:23). While many nations will reject God and his ways, some will follow. Hope remains for the nations.

We also see God's love for the nations in the final chapters of Revelation. In the heavenly city we are told that the nations will walk in the light that comes from the glory of God and the Lamb. The kings of the earth will bring their splendor into the city, and the glory and honor of the nations will be brought into the city (21:23–26). God's multicultural people in the new creation fulfills the long-standing promise to Abraham to create from him a people as numerous as the stars of the sky, the dust of the earth, and the sand of the seashore (Gen 12:2–3; 13:16; 15:5; 22:17).[3] In contrast to the ungodly nations who once brought their wealth into Babylon (Rev 18:11–16), the redeemed nations will now bring themselves, their gifts, and their resources into the new Jerusalem. Images of worship and praise now replace images of consumerism and idolatry.

In the heavenly garden city described in Revelation 22, the tree of life grows on either side of the river of living water that flows from God's throne through the city. While the term "tree" is singular, the fact that it grows on both sides of the river suggests it is a collective singular that refers to the trees of life that line both sides of the river (see the same reality in Ezek 47:12).

But John mentions the one tree of life because he's also likely thinking about the one tree of life in the garden of Eden. He doesn't care so much about geographical precision as much as getting across his theological point: God's people will be totally surrounded and engulfed by God's life—one tree of life that grows along both sides of the river of life, combining Ezekiel and Genesis.

The really cool thing about this tree as it relates to the nations is the leaves. The prophet Ezekiel spoke about the heavenly city and the trees of life and noted that their leaves were for healing (Ezek 47:12). But John adds a phrase: "the leaves of the tree are for the healing *of the nations*" (Rev 22:2). The addition of the healing "of the nations" shows again that God plans to have a multicultural people in his heavenly city. What God has done in Christ is specifically for the salvation or healing of the nations.

God loves the nations. Most of us tend to be very comfortable with our own culture: the way we prepare and eat food; how we celebrate; what we prize and what we despise; our language, television shows, favorite politicians, as well as almost everything related to how we do church. It's a shock for some to realize that there is truth and beauty and goodness among Christians from different cultures. God forbid that we should have to admit that some things are actually done better in other cultures!

Our mission connects directly to God's heart for the nations. At the end of the Gospels, Jesus commands the apostles to "make disciples of all nations" (Matt 28:19), a commission that probably shocked many of them. The book of Acts reports how this mission unfolds as the commission is repeated (Acts 1:8), the Holy Spirit comes on Christ followers of all races (Acts 2; 8; 10), and the apostle Paul begins mission work to the ends of the earth (Acts 13–28). Pastor and author Kent Hughes tells how we sometimes miss grand opportunities for the gospel when our hearts don't beat in rhythm with God's heart:

Mahatma Gandhi shares in his autobiography that in his student days in England he was deeply touched by reading the Gospels and seriously considered becoming a convert to Christianity, which seemed to offer a real solution to the caste system that divided the people of India. One Sunday he attended church services and decided to ask the minister for enlightenment on salvation and other doctrines. But when Gandhi entered the sanctuary, the ushers refused to give him a seat and suggested that he go elsewhere to worship with his own people. He left and never came back. "If Christians have caste differences also," he said to himself, "I might as well remain a Hindu!"[4]

Since God loves the nations, our mission now must include the nations. He calls us to love people of all cultures, just as he does. He calls us to share the good news of Jesus Christ with all peoples. He calls us to be intentional about forming multicultural churches now as a prelude to the coming heavenly reality. He calls us to affirm how other believers worship and how they express their faith. He calls us to accept believers from other cultures into our churches and community groups and circles of friendship. The oft-quoted saying by the Reverend Martin Luther King Jr. that "eleven o'clock on Sunday morning is one of the most segregated hours, if not the most segregated hours, in Christian America"[5] continues to haunt us and should deeply convict us. We can't love God and not care about the nations he loves. When we love God, we will care about the people he cares about—the people of all nations. Someone at some point loved us in the name of Jesus, and we are to love because he first loved us (1 John 4:19).

Jesus, the Faithful Witness

Revelation ties our mission to the nations strongly to Jesus as the faithful witness. The two are inseparable. The opening greeting of Revelation reads like this (1:4–6):

John, To the seven churches in the province of Asia: Grace and peace to you from him who is, and who was, and who is to come, and from the seven spirits before his throne, and from Jesus Christ, who is the faithful witness, the firstborn from the dead, and the ruler of the kings of the earth. To him who loves us and has freed us from our sins by his blood, and has made us to be a kingdom and priests to serve his God and Father—to him be glory and power for ever and ever! Amen.

Jesus is the faithful witness because he is the authoritative witness to God's ways and truth who exposes the lies of Satan. In 3:14, Jesus speaks as the "Amen, the faithful and true witness," and stands in contrast to the unfaithful witnesses of the Laodicean church. In other words, Jesus lives and speaks God's truth rather than lining up with the values and views of this world's system. Out of his mouth comes the sharp, double-edged sword to rebuke and correct his followers (1:16; 2:12, 16) and to judge the wicked (19:11, 15, 21).

The supreme expression of Jesus's witness was his obedience unto death on a cross (see "from the dead" and "by his blood" in 1:4–6 above). He was deemed worthy to take the scroll and open its seals because he was slain, and with his blood he "purchased for God persons from every tribe and language and people and nation" (5:9). At the beginning of chapter 5, John hears about the mighty Lion of the tribe of Judah, who has triumphed (5:5), but when he turns to see the lion, he actually sees a Lamb "looking as if it had been slain" (5:6). Jesus fulfilled his mission through his redemptive sacrifice on our behalf.

Surely our mission should imitate Jesus's mission in some ways. We know that Jesus's cross and resurrection were unique, but we also hear Jesus telling us to deny ourselves, take up our cross, and follow him (e.g., Mark 8:34). Our witness loses something significant when we fail to imitate Jesus. When we rely on human might and power to accomplish our God-given mission—whether military, economic, political, or religious—we are losing from the start. We must accomplish our mission through service, sacrifice, prayer, forgiveness, speaking the truth in love, and other Christlike means. Beware of trying to accomplish God's mission using worldly strategies. Ultimately, that approach will come crashing down. Through the example of Jesus, the Lion-Lamb, God has already shown us that his power is made perfect in human weakness (Rev 12:11; 2 Cor 12:9–10).

The Church as a Community of Faithful Witnesses

Our mission comes into sharp focus in Revelation 11 with John's vision of the two witnesses. Revelation 10:1–11:13 is an interlude that speaks to the situation of God's people in this world. John is told to continue his prophetic ministry (10:1–11), and then we see the entire church called to join in that prophetic ministry (11:1–13). Although chapter 11 is a bit complicated and difficult to interpret, I'm persuaded that the entire temple represents the people of God, but from two different perspectives. The inner court is measured, a symbol here of protection against spiritual attack, but the outer court is unmeasured, here meaning lack of protection against physical attack. This suggests that while believers are sealed with the Spirit and protected spiritually, they are vulnerable to persecution and even martyrdom. The two witnesses represent the witnessing church. There are two of them because two people were needed to constitute a valid legal testimony (e.g., Num 35:30; Deut 17:6; 19:15; Matt 18:16; 2 Cor 13:1; 1 Tim 5:19). They are also described using images drawn from Zechariah 4, where the two olive trees are empowered by God's Spirit to lead God's people. Here the olive trees are equated with the two lampstands, an image already identified in Rev 1:12, 20 as the people of God.[6]

In Revelation 10, John eats the scroll, and although it tastes sweet in his mouth, it turns his stomach bitter, meaning that while God's plan is being fulfilled (sweet), the victory will come through the faithful sacrifice and suffering of his people (bitter) as they bear witness to Jesus in a hostile world.

Revelation 11 essentially tells us three things about being a witness: (1) we are called to live and speak prophetically (i.e., to *be* witnesses), (2) we should be willing to suffer as part of our witness, and (3) God will protect us spiritually and ultimately vindicate us as his people.[7]

First, we are called to live and speak prophetically. Like the prophets of old, we are called to be God's truth tellers, speaking forth his character and ways. In 11:5–6 notice that the power of the witnesses lies in their word. But since God's will often runs counter to the prevailing views of this world, the witnesses have been empowered to speak forth (or prophesy) God's truth and coming judgment for those who rebel against God. This is our task as well. This is certainly not the way to win a popularity contest in a world that bleeds political correctness. But this is part of our calling. If we remember that God's will is also our highest good, it makes more sense. I can hear the echo of Jesus's parting words to his disciples: "But you will receive power when the Holy Spirit comes on you; and you will be my witnesses in Jerusalem, and in all Judea and Samaria, and to the ends of the earth" (Acts 1:8). I think bearing the "testimony of Jesus" or serving as a "faithful witness" to Jesus means telling people about our relationship to Jesus and what he has done as well as imitating Jesus's way of life. It's words *and* actions; both what we say *and* how we live.

I grew up in a church setting that emphasized evangelism almost exclusively. For years I overreacted to an insensitive, guilt-motivated, superficial view of bearing witness to Jesus. A more holistic and biblical view of bearing witness runs much deeper. For people to truly hear what we say about Jesus, they must first see that we live like Jesus. When you read through the seven messages in Revelation 2–3, you get a sense for the kind of life that pleases Jesus. Here is a list from these two chapters: working hard, persevering, refusing to tolerate false teaching, enduring hardships for Christ's sake, suffering persecution, being faithful unto death, refusing to deny Christ under pressure, living faithfully in a difficult spiritual environment, loving, serving, growing spiritually, and keeping Jesus's word. As I try to live and speak prophetically, I find myself praying often for wisdom and discernment and courage. That's always a good place to begin.

Second, being a witness means we should be willing to suffer as part of our witness. Although not the case when Revelation was written, by the second century the Greek word *martys* ("witness") was widely used to refer to martyrdom. We see this play out in Revelation 11 as the witnesses are overpowered and killed by the beast. They are disgraced even more when their bodies are denied a proper burial (11:7–9). In the first-century culture (and much of the world still today) to deny one a proper burial was a sign of insult, shame, and humiliation. The witnesses' humiliating martyrdom is celebrated by the powers of this world (11:10).

The call for witnesses to suffer appears throughout Revelation. In 6:9, John sees under the altar the souls of those who have been slain "because of the word of God and the testimony they had maintained." These Christian martyrs suffered and died specifically because of their witness. In 16:5–6 God is praised for judging those who have "shed the blood of your holy people and your prophets," and in 18:24 we are told that Babylon the Great has spilled "the blood of prophets and of God's holy people, and all who have been slaughtered on the earth." The great prostitute is said in another place to be "drunk with the blood of God's holy people, the blood of those who bore testimony to Jesus" (17:6). One more explicit reference is 20:4, where we are told that John sees the souls of those who have been "beheaded because of their testimony about Jesus and because of the word of God." They have not worshiped false gods and have reserved their allegiance for Jesus alone.

It's true that most of us will not suffer martyrdom, but we might be challenged to suffer in less dramatic but still very tangible and real ways. Such suffering could include ridicule or exclusion or economic punishment. Persecution doesn't have to be physical to be persecution; it can also be economic, social, political, or religious. Nevertheless, Revelation calls us to live a willing-to-die kind of life. Perhaps the greatest calling for those of us not physically threatened is to stay informed about, pray for, and speak out for those who are being persecuted.

I'm reminded of Martin Niemöller, a Lutheran pastor who resisted the Nazis during Hitler's reign of terror. He was imprisoned for eight years in concentration camps and narrowly escaped execution. His words continue to ring true in this context:

> First they came for the Socialists, and I did not speak out—because I was not a Socialist. Then they came for the Trade Unionists, and I did not speak out—because I was not a Trade Unionist. Then they came for the Jews, and I did not speak out—because I was not a Jew. And then they came for me—and there was no one left to speak for me.[8]

Doing nothing simply isn't a Christian option. All of us can at least pray for the persecuted church. Many of us can do more.

The third thing Revelation tells us about being a faithful witness is that God will protect us spiritually and ultimately vindicate us as his people. In Revelation 11 the witnesses are protected by their fiery words that devour their enemies. The witnesses are eventually attacked and killed by the beast. It's reasonable to ask how God protects them when they end up dying as martyrs.

What kind of protection is this? Throughout Revelation, I see the protection as spiritual rather than physical. In 3:10 Jesus makes the church at Philadelphia this promise: "Since you have kept my command to endure patiently, I will also keep you from the hour of trial that is going to come on the whole world to test the inhabitants of the earth." This is a promise of spiritual protection. The same verb and preposition combination ("keep you from," Gk. *tēreō ek*) is used elsewhere only in John 17:15, where Jesus says, "My prayer is not that you take them out of the world but that you *protect* them *from* the evil one" (cf. John 16:33; 2 Pet 2:9).

As we've already mentioned, the seal of the living God in Revelation 7 represents God's spiritual protection of his people. We see his protection again in chapter 12, where the woman (and by implication, her children) symbolizes the people of God. They are protected in the wilderness against the water spewed from the mouth of the dragon. This river of venom represents Satan's lies, deceit, false teaching, slander, accusations, counterfeit miracles, and persecution aimed at destroying God's people.

Although God has promised us spiritual protection, we could still suffer persecution and perhaps martyrdom. Revelation tells us that God plans to vindicate his people once and for all by raising them from the dead and judging their persecutors. Our spiritual protection now leads to our total vindication at the return of Christ. In the meantime, we are disciples, or followers, of the crucified Christ. We have been told to take up our cross and follow him. As Dietrich Bonhoeffer wrote in his book *The Cost of Discipleship*, "When Christ calls a man, he bids him come and die."[9]

Although the witnesses are martyred in 11:7, God raises them from the dead in 11:11–12: "But after the three and a half days the breath of life from God entered them, and they stood on their feet, and terror struck those who saw them. Then they heard a loud voice from heaven saying to them, 'Come up here.' And they went up to heaven in a cloud, while their enemies looked on." The raising up of the witnesses symbolizes the resurrection of the church. It reminds us of the time when God breathes life into the dead bones in Ezekiel 37. Resurrection is God's reversal of the world's verdict of persecution and martyrdom. Through resurrection God defeats evil's greatest and last weapon: death (1 Cor 15:26, 51–57). We need not fear death, because God's vindication includes resurrection from the dead. There comes a time when the mission is complete, when the kingdom of this world will become the kingdom of our Lord and of his Messiah (Rev 11:15), when the Lord's prayer—"your kingdom come, your will be done, on earth as it is in heaven"—becomes reality (Matt 6:10).

God's vindication includes not only the resurrection and rewarding of his people (Rev 11:11–12, 18) but also the judgment of evil (11:17–18). In other words, God doesn't just rescue his people; he also punishes the wicked people and powers that have committed evil acts against his children—unless they repent and turn to Christ. Evildoers do not get away with it. We see in 18:20 that God has judged Babylon "with the judgment she imposed on you." And in 19:2 God, whose judgments are always true and just, has "condemned the great prostitute" and "avenged on her the blood of his servants," those who have been faithful in their witness even to the point of suffering. God will vindicate his people.

The Ethical Life of Faithful Witnesses

While our mission is tied directly to our witness, our witness is not just verbal. Our witness is fundamentally related to how we live, to our actions as well as our words. Our mission is tied up with our ethical or moral life.

In Revelation true believers are actually identified and defined by their faithful lifestyle. Notice how obedience defines who we are in these two passages:

> 12:17: "Then the dragon was enraged at the woman and went off to wage war against the rest of her offspring— those who keep God's commands and hold fast their testimony about Jesus."

14:12: "This calls for patient endurance on the part of the people of God who keep his commands and remain faithful to Jesus."

I don't think we're talking about sinless perfection here, meaning that if we ever disobey or struggle with sin, we can't be part of God's people. But we are talking about the overall direction of a person's life. We are immersed in the struggle, just like the Christians we read about in the seven churches of Revelation 2–3, but are we choosing Jesus above the idols our world offers? Do we believe that he loves us the most and has our best interest at heart? Do we trust that his will is ultimately what is best not only for us but for the whole world? Do we believe that Satan is a liar and that we can't always trust our instincts or urges? Do we live like we believe that Jesus is Lord of lords and King of kings and deserves our worship and obedience?

We see the same kind of defining statements at the beginning and end of the book:

1:3: "Blessed is the one who reads aloud the words of this prophecy, and blessed are those who hear it and take to heart what is written in it, because the time is near."

22:7: "Look, I am coming soon! Blessed is the one who keeps the words of the prophecy written in this scroll."

22:9: "But he said to me, 'Don't do that! I am a fellow servant with you and with your fellow prophets and with all who keep the words of this scroll. Worship God!'"

That's right—we will be blessed if we take to heart (obey) or keep (obey) what is written in Revelation. This may sound harsh to us, but Revelation lays out only two options: being blessed or being cursed.

We also see obedience stressed in the seven messages to the churches in Revelation 2–3:

2:26: "To the one who is victorious and does my will to the end, I will give authority over the nations."

3:3: "Remember, therefore, what you have received and heard; hold it fast, and repent."

3:8: "I know your deeds. See, I have placed before you an open door that no one can shut. I know that you have little strength, yet you have kept my word and have not denied my name."

The ethical life of the witness bearers shines brightly in 14:4–5, where we see the glorious final outcome for God's people, and the redeemed are described in terms of their character and behavior: "These are those who did not defile themselves with women, for they remained virgins. They follow the Lamb wherever he goes. They were purchased from among mankind and offered as firstfruits to God and the Lamb. No lie was found in their mouths; they are blameless." When John says they are "virgins," it sounds like he is being disrespectful to both women and marriage, but he is speaking figuratively about important spiritual truths. In light of the contrast in Revelation between ungodly and godly women (e.g., the great prostitute Babylon versus the bride of Christ), and because these women represent large groups of people, the term "virgins" here refers to all genuine believers who have refused to compromise with the world (cf. 19:7–8).[10] The idea of being defiled with women then becomes a symbol of spiritual adultery (14:8; 17:1–5; 18:3). In other words, faithful witnesses reserve themselves for one spiritual husband: Jesus.

The colorful description in the first part of 14:4 gives way to a straightforward description later in the verse: "They follow the Lamb wherever he goes." You're looking at one of the clearest definitions of discipleship in the whole Bible. Our mission first and foremost is to be Jesus followers. Unless we do that, little else matters.

As people redeemed by the blood of the Lamb, we belong exclusively to the Lord. Our desire is to speak without lies or deceit. You might say we are ambassadors of truth and enemies of falsehood in what we say and how we live. In this sense, John describes Jesus followers as "blameless" (14:5), a word that emphasizes the moral and ethical integrity of God's people (Eph 1:14; 5:27; Phil 2:15; Col 1:22–23; Heb 9:14; 1 Pet 1:19; Jude 24).

In this section, we are reminded that our mission is tied to how we live as well as what we say. Sadly, I will never forget as a college student going out to lunch with a prominent evangelist. By prominent, I mean one of the most popular, effective evangelists anywhere. As we sat there, I was shocked and saddened and confused by his repeated derogatory comments about the waitress. It was as if someone were saying yes and shaking his head no at the same time. I'll never forget how, as a college kid who wanted to walk with the Lord, I was confused and repulsed by the hypocrisy. I simply couldn't process the mixed messages. Bearing witness certainly means speaking about Jesus, but it also means living like Jesus. Words and actions are like the two wings of an airplane—both are essential.

Persevering in the Mission

Revelation makes one additional but supersignificant point: we must persevere in the mission. This shows up most powerfully as you look at the word "overcome," or "conquer," throughout the book, which we will do in a later chapter. But I need to say just a few words about perseverance here.

John has been exiled to Patmos because of the word of God and the testimony about Jesus (1:9). He is an old man who has been a key leader in the early church for many years. Now at the end of his life, he's been relegated to a tiny island in the middle of nowhere to live out his days in exile. So much for climbing the ladder of success. It doesn't exactly match the American dream, does it? Many early Christian leaders faced similar types of suffering.

What's more, John tells his readers in the same verse: "I [am] . . . your brother and companion in the suffering and kingdom and patient endurance that are ours in Jesus" (1:9). So this idea of enduring to the end, even if it means exile or imprisonment or martyrdom or some other undesirable situation, doesn't just apply to John; it also applies to us.

Likewise, Jesus commends certain churches for their perseverance in the seven messages. To the church in Ephesus he says, "I know your deeds, your hard work and your perseverance. . . . You have persevered and have endured hardships for my name, and have not grown weary" (2:2–3). To the church in Thyatira he says, "I know your deeds, your love and faith, your service and perseverance, and that you are now doing more than you did at first" (2:19). And to the Philadelphian Christians he says, "Since you have kept my command to endure patiently, I will also keep you from the hour of trial that is going to come on the whole world to test the inhabitants of the earth" (3:10).

Finally, in Revelation 12–14, there are two specific places where perseverance is highlighted. First, in chapter 13 after the beast is introduced and we're told he will conquer the saints for a time, John writes: "'If anyone is to go into captivity, into captivity they will go. If anyone is to be killed with the sword, with the sword they will be killed.' This calls for patient endurance and faithfulness on the part of God's people" (13:10). Second, after being advised of the punishment awaiting the wicked, God's people are exhorted once again to persevere in 14:12: "This calls for patient endurance on the part of the people of God who keep his commands and remain faithful to Jesus."

Let's be honest—it's hard to persevere in the mission at times. Discouragement can come from unexpected quarters and at unexpected times. It's tempting to lose heart. I've been there.

What often helps me is to pray hard for the strength and grace to persevere. Prayer is the language of perseverance. When you pour out your heart to God in reverent honesty, good things happen. Sometimes God changes our situation, while at other times he changes our perspective and renews us by his Spirit. If you're struggling to stay faithful, pray and keep on praying like your life depends on it.

Conclusion

We are still on this earth for a reason. We have a mission to fulfill, and it begins with God's love for the nations, for the people who are susceptible to Satan's deceptive schemes but also within reach of God's love and the good news of Jesus Christ. Our task is to bear witness to God and the Lamb through our actions and our words to all peoples. Jesus is our example of what it means to be a faithful witness, so, as the writer of Hebrews puts it, "let us run with perseverance the race marked out for us, fixing our eyes on Jesus, the pioneer and perfecter of faith" (Heb 12:1–2).

We bear witness as a community of faith, not merely as individual believers. Revelation 11 helps us see our opportunities and responsibilities as witnesses: to live and speak prophetically, to be willing to suffer as part of our mission, and to rely on God's spiritual protection and ultimate vindication.

Here is the pressing question: To what extent are we engaged in the mission of the church, clarified by the book of Revelation? I'll admit that my focus tends to be much less grand. I'm usually consumed with balancing the checkbook, buying groceries, mowing the yard, spending time with family, riding my Trek, and so on. It's easy to begin thinking that either we are engaged in twenty-four-hour, nonstop witnessing to lost people and pretend that ordinary life doesn't exist *or* we are consumed with ordinary life to the neglect of the mission. Again, having grown up in a kind of either-or culture when it comes to witnessing, I've spent a lot of time thinking about and wrestling with this issue. I've come to the conclusion that it's not really the mission or life but the mission through life. Jesus's Great Commission begins, "Go and make disciples," a statement that could be translated, "As you go, make disciples" (Matt 28:19). When we separate our mission from our life, we lose, and so does the mission.

We have the greatest of callings—to be a faithful witness to Jesus and to the life he offers. As we go about life, may we become more aware and more intentional and more courageous and more Spirit-led in fulfilling our God-given mission.

Key texts: Rev 1:3; 6:9; 10:9–11; 14:4–5; 17:6; 20:4; 22:2, 17
Reading plan: Revelation 10–11; 14

Community Group Questions

1. How does your local community of faith reflect the "every tribe, language, people, and nation" mind-set of Revelation? What seems to be the greatest obstacle(s) to a multicultural community in your context?

2. What motivates you to be concerned about the nations? How can we be more effective in reaching the nations?

3. As you seek to imitate Jesus, the faithful witness, how do you see God's power being made perfect in your weakness?

4. When we talk about living and speaking prophetically, what lessons have you learned that would prove helpful to others?

5. How much are we really prepared to suffer as part of carrying out our mission? What works against a willing-to-suffer mentality?

6. How can your friends pray specifically for you as you seek to "follow the Lamb wherever he goes"?

7. Faithful witnesses endure or persevere. What are the greatest challenges to perseverance in your life right now?

7

JESUS CHRIST
"The Lamb, Who Was Slain"

From cover to cover, Revelation is all about Jesus. Ancient authors often provided the title of the book and a summary of its contents in the opening line, and Revelation follows suit: "The revelation from Jesus Christ" (1:1). The Greek term *apokalypsis* ("revelation") refers to something unveiled, revealed, or made known. Revelation relates to what happens at the end of history, to be sure, but first and foremost it's a book about Jesus. It tells us who he is, what he has done, and what he will do. We learn that Jesus is one with God and shares with him the throne of the universe. We see how he carried out God's plan as the Lamb of God by dying on the cross for our sins and being raised from the dead. We read of his presence among the churches as the Shepherd Messiah, who knows and cares for his people. We take hope in his promise to return as the Warrior Judge to conquer evil (the Lamb is also the Lion) but also as the Bridegroom coming for his bride, the church. Think of it this way: Revelation gives us the theological icing on the cake of the Jesus story provided in the four Gospels. Jesus is the main theme of Revelation.

Jesus Christ Is God

We begin with something we need to believe about Jesus: he is God and is one with the Father and the Holy Spirit. Revelation's Christology (the part of theology that studies who Jesus Christ is and what he has done) is extremely exalted, meaning that the book1 portrays Jesus as fully God and totally one with God. As one prominent theologian puts it, "The importance of John's extraordinarily high Christology for the message of Revelation is that it makes absolutely clear that what Christ does, God does."[1] In other words, what we hear Jesus saying and doing, both in saving his people and in judging the wicked and defeating Satan, this is exactly what God Almighty is saying and doing.

This is exceptionally important to believe because in our day there are many who say that Jesus might have been a respectable religious teacher but was and is nowhere close to being one with God. He might be a powerful prophet, an important historical figure, and even a charismatic miracle worker, but he's not God. Revelation begs to differ by insisting in a variety of ways that Jesus is completely one with God. What Christ does, God does.

We see Jesus's oneness with God when he is mentioned as a member of the Trinity (1:4–5):

> John, To the seven churches in the province of Asia: Grace and peace to you from him who is, and who was, and who is to come [*God the Father*], and from the seven spirits before his throne [*God the Holy Spirit*], and from Jesus Christ [*God the Son*], who is the faithful witness, the firstborn from the dead, and the ruler of the kings of the earth.

We see this again in 5:6, when John sees the slain Lamb standing at the center of God's throne. Here Jesus, the Lamb, has seven horns and seven eyes, which are the seven spirits of God (i.e., the sevenfold Holy Spirit) sent out into all the earth. You can't really be a member of the Trinity without being God and one with God.

It's also fascinating to notice that in Revelation Jesus shares many of the titles used for God:

Title/Description	God the Father	Jesus Christ, God the Son
Was, is, is to come	1:4, 8; 4:8 (partial in 11:17; 16:5)	Coming soon—1:7; 22:7, 12, 20
Alpha and Omega	1:8; 21:6	22:13
First and Last		1:17; 22:13
Beginning and End	21:6	22:13

Jesus's oneness with God is also stressed in a lot of other ways. For instance, in 1:12–16 John's description of Jesus uses powerful images taken from Daniel 7 and 10, where these same features are connected to the "Ancient of Days" (God). As mentioned above, Jesus also shares God's throne in Revelation, showing his unique oneness with God. There is only one throne of God in Revelation, and he shares it with the Lamb (see 3:21; 5:6; 7:17; 22:1, 3). Don't get sidetracked by the logistics of how two people can sit on one throne—that's not John's point. He's telling us that Jesus is God.

The Father's name and the Lamb's name are also connected. When Jesus stands on Mount Zion with the 144,000, they are said to have the Lamb's name and the Father's name written on their foreheads (14:1; also 3:12). In addition, just as God pours out his wrath against evil, so also does Jesus (6:16–17; see also 19:15): "They called to the mountains and the rocks, 'Fall on us and hide us from the face of him who sits on the throne and from the wrath of the Lamb! For the great day of their wrath has come, and who can withstand it?'"

I don't often warn you in this book, but I need to at this point. Beware of any person (no matter how popular or powerful) or church or group or movement that makes Jesus out to be less than God. Revelation (and the rest of the New Testament) makes it crystal clear that Jesus Christ is God. Bad theology hurts people, and denying Jesus's oneness with God, the same thing as denying Jesus's deity, has devastating eternal consequences.

All this information taken together tells us that Jesus, God the Son, is totally one with God the Father and God the Spirit. He's not merely a cool guy worthy of necklaces, tattoos, and movies. He's worthy of worship as God. We finish this section by seeing how Jesus shares the worship reserved for God alone.

In Revelation we are called to worship the Lamb alongside God the Father. In 4:8–11, the worship of God as the Creator is followed by the worship of Jesus as Redeemer in 5:9–12. Chapters 4–5 conclude with this chorus of praise: "Then I heard every creature in heaven and on earth and under the earth and on the sea, and all that is in them, saying: 'To him who sits on the throne and to the Lamb be praise and honor and glory and power, for ever and ever!'" (5:13).

As the story of Revelation moves to the heavenly city in chapters 21–22, the worship of God and the Lamb comes closer and becomes even more personal as believers experience his glorious presence. "The Lord God Almighty and the Lamb" are the temple of the heavenly city (21:22). "The glory of God" gives the city light, and "the Lamb is its lamp" (21:23). The river of the water of life flows "from the throne of God and of the Lamb" (22:1). In 22:3, God and the Lamb share the throne, and his servants will "serve" (or "worship") him. Many of these themes come together in 7:15–17 with the description of the great multitude in heaven:

> Therefore, "they are before the throne of God and serve [same Greek word for "worship" as in 22:3 (see CEV)] him day and night in his temple; and he who sits on the throne will shelter them with his presence. 'Never again will they hunger; never again will they thirst. The sun will not beat down on them,' nor any scorching heat. For the Lamb at the center of the throne

will be their shepherd; 'he will lead them to springs of living water.' 'And God will wipe away every tear from their eyes.'"

Revelation echoes Jesus's statement in John 10:30: "I and the Father are one." For the early Christians, who were committed monotheists, to worship Jesus alongside God means only one thing: they saw Jesus as God. What Christ does, God does.

Jesus Is the Shepherd Messiah

At times Jesus is shown to be the mighty Warrior Judge bent on destroying evil, and so he is. But he is also portrayed in Revelation as the Shepherd Messiah, who knows and cares deeply for his people. We see this in the opening chapter right after John has his vision of the risen Christ in all his glory (read 1:10–16). After encountering Christ, John falls down as if he's dead. He's terrified and speechless. But Jesus quickly reassures him with words that show his shepherd's heart (1:17–18):

- "Do not be afraid"—John must stop being afraid of the one he serves. Fear can melt away because of who Jesus is and what he has done.
- "I am"—This is an allusion to the divine name in Exod 3:14.
- "The First and the Last"—Jesus is the eternal Lord of all.
- "The Living One . . . keys of death and Hades"—Jesus is the resurrected and living Lord, who has conquered death and the grave and now holds power and authority over that realm.

That's pretty encouraging. If you're wondering if these words apply to us as well, the same risen Christ who spoke to John also stands among the seven golden lampstands (the seven churches) and speaks to them (and to us). At the beginning of each letter, Jesus tells the church that he "knows" their situation.

For some this is extremely convicting because they can't hide their sin from the all-knowing Lord. But more often than not, it's comforting: "I know your deeds, your hard work and your perseverance" (2:2), or "I know your afflictions and your poverty" (2:9), or "I know where you live—where Satan has his throne" (2:13), or "I know your deeds, your love and faith, your service and perseverance, and that you are now doing more than you did at first" (2:19), or "I know that you have little strength, yet you have kept my word and have not denied my name" (3:8). Jesus walks among his people and knows his people intimately, like the perfect shepherd protecting and caring for his sheep.

How ironic that the Lamb is also the Shepherd. He is the slain-but-risen Lamb, which means that he knows what it feels like to suffer and die. As the prophet Isaiah put it long ago when prophesying about the Messiah, "He was despised and rejected by mankind, a man of suffering, and familiar with pain" (Isa 53:3). As the suffering Messiah, Jesus is intimately familiar with pain and injustice and suffering. John begins the whole book by referring to the "suffering and kingdom and patient endurance that are ours in Jesus," meaning that we experience such things because we follow Jesus but also that they are part of the path Jesus himself took (Rev 1:9). If you're suffering, know that you follow a Lord who knows what it means to suffer. He hears your deepest cries.

The tremendously good news is that suffering is not the end of the story. Our Shepherd's care now is only a prelude to the total care and provision and protection he will lavish on us one day. First, he plans on getting us to the heavenly city. The vision of Revelation 14 shows the Lamb standing on Mount Zion with the 144,000 (all God's people), no longer in the trenches of spiritual combat but now celebrating their victory by singing a new song. After he leads his people victoriously to the heavenly city, there is the great wedding of the Lamb and his bride. The bride of Christ, the church, has made herself ready and now celebrates her marriage to the perfect Husband (19:7, 9; 21:9). God and the Lamb now shelter their people with their presence (7:15–17).

God's name often symbolizes God's presence in Revelation. In the heavenly city, the throne of God and the Lamb will take center stage, and his servants will see his face, and his name will be on their foreheads (22:3–4; also 3:12; 14:1). Those bearing the name of God and the Lamb will also have their names written in the Lamb's book of life (21:27). Along with presence comes absolute and total security. We belong to him, and we will live forever in a secure relationship with Jesus, the Shepherd, who laid down his life for the sheep (John 10:11; 1 John 3:16).

As the perfect Shepherd, Jesus will not just be with us; he will also provide for us. Again, in Revelation 7, also a vision of the heavenly city, we are told that God's people will never again suffer hunger or thirst or scorching heat. Instead, the Lamb will be their Shepherd and will "lead them to springs of living water" (7:17). The final scene of the heavenly city also shows the river of the water of life flowing from the throne of God and of the Lamb (22:1). Water in a hot, dry climate such as the Middle East is a huge deal. Water means life. That is what is being communicated. Jesus provides life!

As we journey toward the heavenly city and the heavenly rewards Jesus has in store, Revelation reminds us of his sustaining grace that is ours here and now. The book opens with the greeting, "Grace and peace to you" from the triune God (1:4). And the book closes, "The grace of the Lord Jesus be with God's people. Amen" (22:21). That's just like our Shepherd—he knows and cares for us now, he promises us future rewards, and he offers us grace and peace all along the way.

The Slaughtered Lamb

One thing that jumps out at you as you read Revelation is that Jesus isn't called "Jesus" or "Christ" very often. Instead, he is usually referred to as "the Lamb." A lamb? Really? Not exactly what you would expect when reading about the Lord of the universe. But Jesus doesn't follow the same conquering path as most superheroes. He conquers the kingdom of darkness in an unexpected manner—through his death.

In Revelation 1, we hear that Jesus "freed us from our sins by his blood" (1:5). The word "freed" (Gk. *lyō*) here means to release or untie someone from what restrains them—Jesus cut us loose from our sins, which held us captive. He did this "by his blood," referring to his sacrificial death on the cross. Blood represents life, so you could say that Jesus gave his life for us. He is the Passover Lamb, whose death made possible our salvation. He took our place and died the death we deserved to die. It was John the Baptist who announced, "Look, the Lamb of God, who takes away the sin of the world!" (John 1:29; cf. 1 Cor 5:7). We are even told that he "was slain from the creation of the world" (Rev 13:8), meaning that God's plan has always been to use the life, death, and resurrection of Jesus to rescue people from sin and Satan.

The picture comes into even sharper focus in Revelation 5. John hears about the Lion of the tribe of Judah, who has triumphed, but he turns to see "a Lamb, looking as if it had been slain, standing at the center of the throne" (5:6). The Lamb looks as if it had been slaughtered, because he had been—on the cross. But he's no longer dead. He's been resurrected and now shares the throne of the universe with God the Father. Jesus receives worship because of his crucifixion, resurrection, and exaltation to the very throne of God: "And they sang a new song, saying: 'You are worthy to take the scroll and to open its seals, because you were slain, and with your blood you purchased . . .'" (5:9) and "In a loud voice they were saying: 'Worthy is the Lamb, who was slain'" (5:12).

Only when we come face-to-face with sin in all its ugliness do we feel an overwhelming gratitude that Jesus died for us, that he died to take away *our* sins, to untie us and set us free. Only when we get to the place where we realize that we deserved death because of our sin and that God gave us life instead do we give thanks to the slain Lamb of God. Only then does worship really make sense.

One very surprising thing about Jesus the victor or conqueror is that he conquered *by being conquered*. That's right—he won, or triumphed (Gk. *nikaō*), by dying a sacrificial death (5:5). No Roman emperor or American general or any worldly leader would conquer like that. You don't conquer by being conquered. You don't win by losing. But Jesus did. He undermined evil. He turned evil inside out. By dying a sacrificial death as the spotless Lamb of God, he took our judgment and gave us forgiveness in its place: "He [God] was unwilling to act in love at the expense of his holiness or in holiness at the expense of his love. So we may say that he satisfied his holy love by himself dying the death and so bearing the judgment which sinners deserved. He both exacted and accepted the penalty of human sin."[2] The genius and beauty of the cross is that it wasn't so much God forcing Jesus to die or God punishing Jesus but God the Son voluntarily submitting to death. What God required, God supplied. God gave himself for us on the cross. John Stott refers to Jesus's death on the cross as the "self-substitution of God," and so it was.[3]

It gets better. Jesus's work doesn't just extend into the past and deal with our sin. His victory on the cross also qualifies him to open the scroll in Revelation 5. The scene opens with John seeing a scroll in God's right hand, a scroll that represents God's redemptive plan to defeat evil once and for all, to rescue his people, and to transform his creation. God isn't just sitting by passively in heaven while this broken world self-destructs. He is doing something about it. God holds the scroll firmly in his right hand, and the heavenly worshipers fall silent as the mighty angel asks, "Who is worthy to break the seals and open the scroll?" (5:2). We come to a critical point in the drama as John weeps in despair when no one in all creation is found worthy to open the scroll (5:3–4). No one can unroll God's plan. The scene intensifies until at last John's hopelessness gives way to the good news of a Conqueror (5:5). There is one who is worthy after all. John's head is spinning for sure as he hears about a lion and then turns to see a once-slaughtered but now fully alive Lamb (5:6).

Jesus, the Lamb of God, is the only one who can take the scroll from the Father (5:2–7), because he alone is the crucified and resurrected Lord. His worthiness results from his faithfulness unto death on the cross. He is capable to carry out God's plan, because he humbled himself unto death. That's why so much of the praise in Revelation begins with "You are worthy . . ."

Let's bring this into our individual world for a second. Only Jesus is worthy, because only he was crucified and resurrected. Only Jesus is Lord of lords and King of kings. It's easy for religious leaders—pastors, teachers, speakers, authors, activists, and so on—to find themselves being elevated by people to a place reserved only for Jesus. They can drift slowly from representing God to replacing God in the hearts of their followers. But we must always remember that only Jesus is authoritatively qualified to fulfill God's plan. Leaders are essential but replaceable; only Jesus is indispensable and irreplaceable.

Jesus's death has done two other things that deeply impact us. First, through his sacrifice he "purchased for God persons from every tribe and language and people and nation" and has "made them to be a kingdom and priests to serve our God, and they will reign on the earth" (5:9–10; also 1:5–6). Christ's work has brought us into a community of faith that God is in the process of making into something amazingly special. It's not just about what God saves us from; it's also about what he saves us for. God has done more than change our relationship to sin; he also changes our present and our future relationships to him and to each other. He saved us to become something, namely, a community or kingdom of priests, who will reign with him in the coming new heaven and new earth.

Second, Christ's work destroys the work of the devil and allows us to conquer him as well. Revelation 12:7–9 reports on a war in heaven between Michael and his angels and the dragon (the devil) and his angels. The devil loses and, along with his demonic angels, is hurled down to earth. Exactly when this occurred is a matter of debate, but Jesus's crucifixion and resurrection are the pivotal victory in this cosmic battle. When Jesus obeyed unto death and God raised him from the dead, Satan was once and for all defeated. We are then told in 12:11 that "they [believers] triumphed over him [the devil] by the blood of the Lamb." When Satan accuses you of being a worthless piece of junk and attempts to deceive you with some fleeting pleasure, remember that you can resist the devil because he's a defeated (although still dangerous) enemy. He has already lost the cosmic war.

The Firstborn from the Dead

Jesus's death would mean nothing without his resurrection. Tens of thousands of people were crucified in the first-century Roman world, but only one was raised from the dead. Revelation mentions resurrection only a few times but everywhere assumes that Jesus is the risen Christ.

In 1:5 we read that Jesus is the "firstborn from the dead." Because of his resurrection, Jesus now rules over death (cf. Col 1:18). In 1:17–18, Jesus tells John not to be afraid, because "I am the Living One; I was dead, and now look, I am alive for ever and ever! And I hold the keys of death and Hades." To the church in Smyrna, Jesus identifies himself as "the First and the Last, who died and came to life again" (2:8). In 5:6, John sees "a Lamb, looking as if it had been slain, standing at the center of the throne." The phrase "as if it had been slain" means "that appeared to have been killed" (NET) or "as if it had once been killed" (CEV). What a paradoxical statement! He saw a slaughtered Lamb . . . standing, meaning the Lamb had been slain or killed but is now very much alive and reigning over the world. He is the sovereign Lord over death. What's more, Jesus's resurrection guarantees our own future resurrection from the dead (1 Cor 15:20).

As I mentioned earlier, for the last two years at our university, we've had a student die. It's painful beyond words, and I find myself telling God over and over how much I hate death, the thief of life. I can always hear his response echoed through his Word in passages like these. At the end of Revelation we read, "Then death and Hades [the grave, or realm of the dead] were thrown into the lake of fire. The lake of fire is the second death" (20:14). I delight in knowing that one day God will send death to hell. In the new heaven and new earth, "there will be no more death" (21:4). The final banishment of death is made possible by the resurrection of Jesus.

The Roaring Lamb

As I write, it seems as if the world is falling apart—Israel and Hamas are at war; a measles outbreak in the US has resulted in more than 300 cases and at least one US city declaring a state of emergency; heavy fighting continues between Syria's forces and the terrorist group ISIS—the same group that has forced 125,000 Christians to flee their homeland in Iraq; and so much more. By the time this book is actually printed there will be other world crises. It's a huge mess. Much of the suffering in the world can be traced immediately (and all of it ultimately) to sin and Satan. Thankfully, Revelation portrays

Jesus not only as one with God, as the Shepherd Messiah, as the slain Lamb, and as the Living One, but also as the Warrior Judge, the roaring Lion and conquering Ram, who will return to demolish evil once and for all. Part of fixing this broken world is getting rid of evil, and Jesus will do just that.

Revelation features a war or combat theme. It's a book about spiritual warfare. We see battle images throughout the seven messages in chapters 2–3: the faithful will receive the "victor's crown" (2:10); Jesus wields a "sharp, double-edged sword" (1:16); Jesus "will fight against [his enemies] with the sword of [his] mouth" (2:16); Jesus "will strike her children dead" (2:23); those who are victorious "will rule with an iron scepter" (2:27); Jesus will make his enemies "come and fall down at your feet" (3:9); Jesus will rule over creation (3:14); and at the end of each message Jesus promises rewards to those who are "victorious." That's a lot of battle imagery. It continues through the rest of the book.

Several times in Revelation we are told plainly that Jesus is the ruler above all rulers. There are a lot of very powerful people in this world and a lot of dangerous unseen spiritual forces, but none can rival Jesus. He is "the ruler of the kings of the earth" (1:5). When the ten kings go to war against the Lamb and his army in chapter 17, they are defeated because Jesus is "Lord of lords and King of kings" (17:14). When Jesus returns, he carries the title on his robe: "KING OF KINGS AND LORD OF LORDS" (19:16).

As ruler of all, Jesus is also the Judge who wages war against evil and wins. Two images stand out. First, he is "the Lion of the tribe of Judah" (5:5; cf. Gen 49:9–10). This refers back to Jacob's blessing over his son Judah, identifying the tribe of Judah as the royal line and here signifying Jesus's power and strength as a mighty warrior and ruler.

The second image is even more fascinating. We know about Jesus as the Lamb, but how about Jesus as the Ram? In 5:6, we see that the Lamb has seven horns and seven eyes, symbolic of his perfect strength and penetrating insight. The Lamb with horns is the Ram. He is both the sacrificial Lamb who died for our sins and also the conquering Ram who judges sin. This explains why the Lamb can also wage war (17:14) and why the wicked will hide in caves and cry out for death in an attempt to escape the coming wrath of the Lamb (6:16–17). Only those bearing the seal of the living God can withstand the Lamb's/Ram's wrath.

It seems as if every generation leans toward the grace/love/ mercy of God or the holiness/justice/righteousness of God. Now, in our love-starved society, we often overemphasize God's love to the neglect of his holiness. When Jesus returns, how-ever, he will come back not as a docile lamb but as a mighty Warrior Judge. He will return in power to finish off the enemies of God. We dare not attempt to domesticate the Lamb. He comes to destroy his enemies and establish his universal reign. Revelation scholar Robert Mounce warns, "Any view of God that eliminates judgment and his hatred of sin in the interest of an emasculated doctrine of sentimental affection finds no support in the strong and virile realism of the Apocalypse."[4]

When Jesus comes back with the clouds (a symbol of God's glorious presence), "every eye will see him, even those who pierced him," and "all peoples on earth 'will mourn because of him'" (1:7). For those who have opposed Jesus, his return will mean their judgment and, therefore, their sorrow. In Revelation 14, we see Jesus seated on a white cloud with a crown of gold on his head and a sharp sickle in his hand (14:14–16). He is given the go-ahead by God through an angel to commence judging the earth, which he does. Chapter 19 provides the most detail in the book of Revelation about Jesus's awesome return.

God's final victory over evil unfolds in 19:6–20:15. After the announcement of the Lamb's wedding in 19:6–10, we read of Christ's second coming in 19:11–21. Jesus appears as Warrior, Judge, and King, who returns in glory and power to defeat his enemies and establish his universal reign. In 19:11–16 we read of eight attributes and four actions of the Conquering Christ (see table).

In 19:17–21, the famous battle of Armageddon occurs (see also 16:14–16). This well-advertised battle turns out to be a nonevent. Forget all the uproar about the battle of Armageddon in end-time books and movies and sermons; here is the report of the actual battle in Revelation (19:20): "but the beast was captured." Christ wins merely by appearing and speaking victory. The epic battle for the future of the universe really occurred in the garden of Gethsemane as Jesus cried out for another way of salvation but yielded to the cross. The turning point in history can be found in Jesus's prayer in that lonely garden: "Not what I will, but what you will" (Mark 14:36). Sin began in a garden, and Satan was defeated in a garden, and as a result, one day we will live in a garden without a trace of evil.

The final piece to the puzzle of Jesus as the roaring Lamb offers us great encouragement. If you're a follower of Jesus and find yourself dreading or fearing his return, Revelation brings relief. You can anticipate, even long for, his return, as a bride eagerly looks forward to her wedding day. Jesus's return won't mean judgment for his people, but rather it will mean rescue, reunion, and reward. Revelation speaks of a time when the kingdom of this world will become the kingdom of our Lord

The Conquering Christ

Attributes	Actions
• Rides a white horse	• Wages war by judging justly
• Faithful and True	• Conquers the nations with the
• Eyes are like blazing fire	sword of his mouth
• Wears many (rulers') crowns	• Conquers the nations with an iron
• Has a name that only he knows	scepter
• Wears a robe dipped in blood	• Treads the winepress of God's furi-
• Name is the Word of God	ous wrath
• Wears the title King of kings and Lord of lords	

and of his Messiah (11:15). Jesus does tell us to be prepared for his return (16:15), but he also promises that it will be a time of reward:

> The nations were angry, and your wrath has come. The time has come for judging the dead, and for rewarding your servants the prophets and your people who revere your name, both great and small—and for destroying those who destroy the earth. (11:18)

> Look, I am coming soon! My reward is with me, and I will give to each person according to what they have done. (22:12)

We can long for Christ's return because we know him as a beloved child knows a trustworthy and loving parent. When the parent is away, the child longs for that parent's return because the child knows the character of the one returning. Our Shepherd Messiah will one day come to rescue us.

Conclusion

I hope you learned something about Jesus in this chapter. But more than that, I hope "the revelation of Jesus Christ" has made you want to love and follow Jesus more (1:1 CSB). Revelation paints a striking picture of Jesus in all his glory. He is one with God. What Christ does, God does. When we deny Jesus's "Godness," as we could call it, we ultimately hurt people by taking them further away from what is true and real.

Jesus is also the Shepherd Messiah, who knows us intimately, empathizes with our suffering, cares for us now, and promises us a new creation that is beyond our grandest imagination. All this is possible because he is the slain Lamb, whose sacrifice on the cross released us from captivity to sin and Satan. Jesus is worthy to unroll the scroll of God's redemptive plan because he is the formerly slaughtered but now resurrected Lamb of God.

As the Lion, conquering Ram, and roaring Lamb, Jesus has defeated Satan through the cross and resurrection. The King of kings and Lord of lords promises to return—a truth that strikes fear in the heart of his enemies and brings chills of hope to his friends.

This world is broken and cannot be fixed apart from Christ's final intervention. We want the kingdom to come in all its fullness. We long for things to be the way they're supposed to be. In the final sentence of Revelation, Jesus promises to return: "He who testifies to these things says, 'Yes, I am coming soon.'" And so our constant prayer remains, "Amen. Come, Lord Jesus" (22:20).

Key texts: Rev 1:1, 4–6, 17–18; 5:5, 9–10; 7:17; 19:11–16; 22:12–13
Reading plan: Revelation 5; 19

Community Group Questions

1. What are some ways that our culture views Jesus as a powerful religious figure but still less than God? How does Revelation challenge those views?

2. To speak of Jesus as the Shepherd Messiah means that he knows and cares for his people. How have you experienced the Shepherd's care recently?

3. Why is it deeply good to reflect often on Jesus's sacrifice for us on the cross? How does the "self-substitution" of God help you understand the cross?

4. What does it mean to you to know that God wasn't just saving you *from* something but also saving you *for* something? What is your favorite promise he has made about the coming new creation?

5. How can you rely on Christ's defeat of Satan to resist the devil's temptations and rebuke his accusations?

6. Why is it important to see Jesus not only as the sacrificial Lamb but also as the conquering Ram who will destroy evil once and for all?

7. How has Revelation changed your understanding of Jesus?

8

JUDGMENT
"How Long, Sovereign Lord?"

One of the worst things you can say about someone today is that they are judgmental. "Stop judging me" or "You shouldn't judge that person" are comments we often hear batted about. Such sentiments come from Christians as well as non-Christians. The "judge not" philosophy is alive and well in our world. Of course, there is some truth to the idea that I'm not your judge and you're not mine, but sometimes we take things too far and transfer those convictions to God, implying that not even God has a right to judge. Let me ask you this: If someone you loved was murdered by someone who would never be apprehended by authorities, would you still want a nonjudgmental God?

Many of us have never faced serious persecution, the kind where you die if you admit to being a Christian. We are, however, becoming more and more aware of the struggle of the persecuted church around the world, and that's good, because we need to pray for them and learn from their examples of faith and courage. It's also important to know that this isn't something new; Christ followers have been persecuted from the beginning. I'm reading through Bryan Litfin's insightful book *Early Christian Martyr Stories*, and the accounts are stunning. Take, for instance, the story of Blandina, a second-century martyr from Lyons:

> After enduring the whips, the fierce animals, and the frying pan, she was finally wrapped in an encumbering net and set before a bull. The creature knocked her around for so long that she lost awareness of her surroundings, thanks to her heavenly hope, her firm grasp on what she believed, and her spiritual intimacy with Christ. At last Blandina was sacrificed, and the pagans were forced to admit that in their experience no woman had ever suffered so many tortures as fearsome as these.[1]

Such an ordeal leaves many of us asking, "Lord, when are you going to judge the people who have committed such horrific acts of evil?" This is precisely what the martyrs are asking in Rev 6:9–10: "When he opened the fifth seal, I saw under the altar the souls of those who had been slain because of the word of God and the testimony they had maintained. They called out in a loud voice, 'How long, Sovereign Lord, holy and true, until you judge the inhabitants of the earth and avenge our blood?'" How long, Lord? You're in control. Surely you won't let evil get away with it. Surely wickedness will not win, will it, Lord. When are you going to judge evil, Lord? Revelation's strong and steady answer is, "No, evil will not win, because God Almighty will defeat and destroy evil."

God's judgment of evil is an outpouring of his wrath. Revelation uses the term "wrath" numerous times, and it's important to know what the term means and what it doesn't mean. Human anger, or wrath, is often impulsive, uncontrolled, and wrongly motivated. We probably all remember a time when we lost it . . . for all the wrong reasons. In contrast, God's anger, or wrath, is always controlled and justified. God's wrath is his intentional condemnation of sin and evil based on his holy and righteous character.

What is it that God is condemning? What kind of evil are we talking about? Three times in Revelation the sins or vices of the wicked are listed: 9:20–21; 21:8; and 22:14–15. We see several types of evil show up repeatedly in the book: worship of false gods (idolatry), sexual immorality, deception, and murder. Human beings engage in such wickedness, human institutions (e.g., the worship system devoted to the Roman emperors) promote it, and demonic powers inspire it. The end result is that God himself is rejected, God's people are persecuted and murdered, God's creation is destroyed, and God's redemptive plan is opposed.

Revelation does not shy away from judgment. You almost get sick of hearing about it, and that's why we must know why it is absolutely essential. The only thing worse than evil would be a God who refuses to condemn it. Through an emphasis on judgment, Revelation reassures us that God will one day completely destroy evil.

God Judges Evil because He Is Holy and Righteous

John F. Kennedy made popular the following quotation that he attributed to the eighteenth-century Irish statesman and philosopher Edmund Burke: "The only thing necessary for the triumph of evil is that good men do nothing." There is a lot of truth to that statement. Everyone deals with the problem of evil, and sometimes it gets pretty personal. When we experience the horrible darkness of evil, we often struggle with God's lack of involvement or intervention. Why didn't God stop it from happening? This is a really important question not to be dismissed quickly, but not one with a simple answer. One part of the biblical answer to the problem of evil is that God is, in fact, in the process of destroying evil. He's not sitting passively on his throne while his people suffer. He is a good God, and he's in the process of judging evil now and will one day remove every last trace of it from his creation. Evil will not win, and the wicked will not get away with it!

Revelation tells us that God's judgment flows out of his character. Because God is holy and righteous, he cannot tolerate evil and must condemn it. We see God's character on display in the great throne-room scene of Revelation 4. The one sitting on the throne has the appearance of jasper and ruby, and an emerald rainbow encircles the throne (4:3). The jeweled description is an attempt to capture the brilliance and splendor of God's holy presence. The Holy Spirit blazes in front of the throne (4:5), a throne surrounded by multitudes of angels who cry out day and night, "'Holy, holy, holy is the Lord God Almighty,' who was, and is, and is to come" (4:8). Then, as Revelation 5 opens, we see our holy and mighty God holding a scroll, which represents his plan for judging evil, redeeming his people, and transforming creation. The scroll has seven seals, and these turn out to be judgments on evil (i.e., the seven seal judgments of chap. 6). No wonder John weeps when no one is found worthy to open the scroll and its seals. The only thing worse than experiencing evil is the thought that evil might get away with it and win in the end. In the midst of John's despair, one of the elders/angels tells him not to cry, because there is a Worthy One: Jesus, the Lamb of God. The Lamb then takes the scroll and opens the seal judgments, the judgments that occur because our holy and just God will not allow evil to win.

We also see that God's righteous character provides the basis for his condemnation of evil in Revelation 15–16. The sea of glass glowing with fire in 15:2 represents God's fiery judgment (cf. 4:6, where the sea of glass symbolizes God's holiness and majesty). God is praised by his victorious people for his great and marvelous deeds and his just and true ways. In other words, God is praised for judging his enemies and rescuing his people, and his judgment of evil flows out of his holy and righteous character: "Who will not fear you, Lord, and bring glory to your name? For you alone are holy" (15:4). The scene then shifts to the preparations for pouring out the last series of judgments against evil, the bowl judgments of chapter 16. The seven bowls are filled with God's wrath against wickedness (15:7). We read in 15:8 that no one can enter the temple until these seven last plagues are completed, signifying that life cannot go on as normal until evil is driven from God's creation. All that God is in himself (love, goodness, justice, holiness, mercy, . . .) simply cannot tolerate evil. God's holy presence and evil will never mix.

At the end of Revelation, we catch a final glimpse of how God's character causes him to judge evil. The last judgment scene occurs in Rev 20:11–15 and is often referred to as the great white throne judgment because of 20:11: "And I saw a great white throne, and sitting upon it was him from whose presence the earth and heavens fled, and there was no place for them" (my translation). God is totally pure, holy, powerful, and sovereign, and before him the wicked must stand in final judgment. Those who rebel against God and reject Jesus Christ will face eternal condemnation. The wicked will not get away with it in the end, even when they appear to get away with it in this life.

Once evil has been eliminated from God's creation, the holy presence of God will envelop his people for eternity. Those who have been judged righteous because of their relationship with Jesus Christ (Rom 8:1), and who have been transformed at their resurrection, will now experience the glorious presence of God up close and personal: "[The angel] showed me the Holy City, Jerusalem, coming down out of heaven from God. It shone with the glory of God, and its brilliance was like that of a very precious jewel, like a jasper, clear as crystal" (21:10–11). We've seen jasper before, when we first heard about God on his throne in 4:3. God's throne is a symbol of his sovereignty, majesty, and glorious presence. Now the glorious presence of God descends to dwell permanently among his people. Because of God's holy and righteous character, he will judge evil and reward his people with his presence.

God, no doubt, has his reasons for delaying the final destruction of evil. As we wait (and sometimes cry out) for God to get rid of evil, he assures us that he will one day destroy evil completely. We see all kinds of evil in this world, and sometimes it happens to us. Sometimes, sadly, we are the doers of evil. In Jesus, we find forgiveness and new life and reconciliation to God. If we reject Jesus, there is no hope for pardon; only judgment remains. Why? Because God is holy and righteous and pure and just, and he cannot tolerate evil.

God Allows Evil to Destroy Itself

Revelation speaks of a final judgment, to be sure, and we'll get to that in a minute, but it also highlights God's ongoing judgment of evil. God doesn't just wait until that last day to begin taking out evil. He condemns wickedness here and now, not always as completely as we would wish, but he definitely begins the process of destroying evil. We see God's present judgment in the first four seal judgments in Rev 6:1–8. These judgments include warfare, violence, bloodshed, economic hardship, and death. Together, they demonstrate some of the disastrous effects of sin that have been around for a while. These are not judgments restricted to the very end of history but are happening now.

What we see with these four seal judgments is that the consequences of sin contain the judgment of God. Notice the expression "was given" used throughout 6:1–8. This is called a divine passive and portrays God as the ultimate source of these judgments (for more on this see "God Is in Control!" in chap. 1). The four riders are given (by God) the judgments on the sins of the nations. As a result, God ultimately stands behind these judgments. We see divine passives also in the series of trumpet judgments: 8:2–3; 9:1, 3–4, 15.

Most important, we see in these judgments that God allows human sin to run its course. Evil will eventually turn on itself and self-destruct. As a former student, Kimberly Carlton, once said, "Evil eats itself." Evil is self-devouring. God's judgment comes when he allows this to occur. We see this in other places in Revelation as well. In 9:3–5, the demonic locusts are given power to torture and bring judgment on wicked human beings. In 17:16–17, God allows the beast to attack and destroy the prostitute, a fulfillment of God's promise to punish the harlot (17:1). That's right—part of God's judgment is for evil powers to turn on each other. Revelation scholar Robert Mounce notes, "The wicked are not a happy band of brothers, but precisely because they are wicked they give way to jealousy and hatred" that results in mutual destruction.[2]

Jesus said that "the thief [Satan] comes only to steal and kill and destroy" (John 10:10), and this includes Satan's desire to destroy unbelievers as well as believers. There is no loyalty among the powers of evil. To Satan, his wicked followers are nothing more than food to be consumed. In *The Screwtape Letters*, C. S. Lewis speaks of the self-devouring nature of evil from a demon's point of view:

> To us [demonic powers] a human is primarily food; our aim is the absorption of its will into ours, the increase of our own area of selfhood at its expense. . . . We want cattle who can finally become food; He [God] wants servants who can finally become sons. We want to suck in, He wants to give out. We are empty and would be filled; He is full and flows over. Our war aim is a world in which Our Father Below has drawn all other beings into himself: the Enemy wants a world full of beings united to Him but still distinct.[3]

God certainly judges directly, but he also judges by allowing evil to run its course and destroy itself. When evil powers and people rebel against God, one aspect of his judgment is to allow them to go their own way, the way of death. We see something similar in Romans 1, where the apostle Paul characterizes the present judgment of God as giving people over to sin: "God gave them over in the sinful desires of their hearts to sexual impurity. . . . God gave them over to shameful lusts. . . . God gave them over to a depraved mind" (Rom 1:24, 26, 28).

We also see a pattern throughout Revelation in how God judges, as New Testament scholar Grant Osborne explains:

> The basic principle of justice in the book is the same legal standard behind both the OT and Roman jurisprudence—*lex talionis*, the law of retribution. It can be stated simply: what you do to others God will do to you. Basically, God allows sin to come full circle and consume itself. The basic law is stated in 2:23, "I will repay each of you according to your deeds."[4]

In Rev 14:8, 10, after Babylon makes "all the nations drink the maddening wine of her adulteries," God forces her to "drink the wine of God's fury, which has been poured full strength into the cup of his wrath." The idea here is that God judges Babylon for her judgment of God's people (see also 18:5–7). In addition, after the third bowl judgment, which turns the waters into blood, God is praised as just and holy for judging those who "have shed the blood of your holy people and your prophets" by giving them "blood to drink as they deserve" (16:5–6). Whereas our judgments are often subject to bad information, favoritism, or our ever-changing emotions, God's judgments are just and true because he is just and true and because he knows perfectly what people have done and why.

When I was little, I spent a week each summer with each set of grandparents. One summer my Granny made pickles. She used lime in the process, and I loved lime—the green flavoring that tasted amazing on snow cones. I pestered her relentlessly for a taste of lime, and she refused, telling me that it wasn't the same lime and it wouldn't taste good. I knew better since I had tasted lime, and it was just sitting there waiting to be enjoyed. The pestering continued until she finally said, "Okay, if you insist, here is a taste of lime." She put a small amount on her finger and let me taste it. I couldn't spit it out fast enough. My own grandmother had poisoned me. But actually, she had just allowed my rebellious choice to run its course. I was suffering the consequences of my own stubborn decision.

One aspect of God's judgment *is* the consequences of sin. We reap what we sow; we harvest what we plant; what goes around, comes around (Gal 6:7). We've seen this in our own lives and in the lives of family members and friends. God is good, and what he gives is good, and what he does is good. He is the source of life. Ultimately, all that is good and life-giving originates with God. So when people reject God and his ways, when they make a bid for independence and claim autonomy, they are really separating themselves from life. Self-reliance results in self-destruction. Revelation stresses that one significant aspect of God's judgment is to allow evil to turn on itself and do its own damage.

God's Judgment Relates to His People

As we saw earlier, Revelation 6 pictures the saints who have been martyred and are now resting under God's protective presence crying out to God: "How long, Sovereign Lord, holy and true, until you judge the inhabitants of the earth and avenge our blood?" (6:10). Revelation teaches that God's judgment of evil connects in some deep ways to the prayers of his people.

In 8:3–5, an angel with a golden censer approaches God's presence. The angel receives incense and the prayers of all God's people to offer on the golden altar in front of God's throne. The smoke from the incense, along with the prayers, floats up to God as a fragrant aroma. The angel then takes the censer, fills it with fire from the altar, and hurls it to earth, an action that results in thunder, lightning, and an earthquake—all symbols of God's judgment. This vision tells us that God most certainly hears the cries of his people for justice and deliverance. The prayers ascend to God, and his judgment descends to the earth. God responds to the prayers of his people with judgment fires from heaven. Those who are suffering and are crying out to God should know that their prayers are being heard and that God's condemnation of evil is a response to hearing their prayers. Prayer is more than thanking God for our food or asking God to help us find a parking spot at church. Revelation encourages believers to cry out for justice and deliverance (e.g., Rom 12:14–21). Our prayers can affect what happens on earth.

Another connection between God's judgment and his people can be found in Revelation 11, where the two witnesses symbolize the witnessing church.[5] The witnesses have tremendous God-given power to bring judgment on their enemies. They do so with fire from their mouths, a symbol of their prophetic message. When we live and speak God's message faithfully and truthfully, the message itself confronts the rebellious world and becomes part of God's judgment on the world. We must always speak the truth in love to be sure (Eph 4:15), but speaking in love doesn't mean that we stop speaking the truth. The message of the cross is offensive and sometimes divisive, but it's also the message of salvation to those who humble themselves and receive God's gift of life. It takes courage and wisdom to speak prophetically, but God promises to empower his people to carry out this difficult assignment. Check out the book of Acts for examples of how God works mightily through his people as they speak prophetically.

The downfall of Babylon the Great in Revelation 18–19 shows us another way in which God's judgments are connected to his people. The first part of chapter 18 describes Babylon's demonic character and adulterous influence. God's people are urged to leave Babylon so as to not experience the coming judgment. Her many sins cluster around blatant materialism and luxury, shameless arrogance and self-glorification, as well as the persecution of God's people. Rev 18:9–19 details Babylon's judgment, and the funeral laments stand in contrast to the rejoicing of God's people in 18:20–19:5. God doesn't judge just wicked people; he also judges evil empires.

God's people are commanded to rejoice at Babylon's downfall. Yes, you read that right. This does not mean delighting in the suffering of sinners, but instead it means celebrating God's justice. Evil rulers and wicked kingdoms that deceive the nations and ruthlessly oppress God's people will be judged: "By your magic spell all the nations were led astray. In her was found the blood of prophets and of God's holy people, of all who have been slaughtered on the earth" (18:23–24). They won't get away with it. When God shows himself faithful by vindicating his people, a celebration is in order: "Rejoice over her, you heavens! Rejoice, you people of God! Rejoice, apostles and prophets! For God has judged her with the judgment she imposed on you" (18:20). The basis of the hallelujah chorus in the first part of Revelation 19 is that God has "condemned the great prostitute who corrupted the earth by her adulteries" and has "avenged on her the blood of his servants" (19:2). God has not ignored evil or let it slide. He's aware of the suffering of his people, and he is doing something about it. At last the prayer of 6:10 is being answered: "How long, Sovereign Lord, . . . until you judge?" As Revelation closes, we see God's people, people who have been judged by the world, now sitting on thrones of judgment, reigning with Christ (3:21; 5:10; 20:4, 6; 22:5).

Visions of Judgment

Revelation also shows us God's coming judgment through colorful and frightening visions and images. In chapter 14, for instance, we have two visions of judgment related to the concept of harvesting: the grain harvest (14:14–16) and the grape harvest (14:17–20). Both visions are tied to Joel 3:13, an Old Testament passage predicting judgment: "Swing the sickle, for the harvest is ripe. Come, trample the grapes, for the winepress is full and the vats overflow—so great is their wickedness!" In the first vision, Jesus is portrayed as "one like a son of man" (14:14) seated on a cloud, wearing a crown and holding a sharp sickle. As the powerful and glorious Judge, Jesus swings the sickle and harvests (or judges) the earth.[6] In the second vision, an angel with a sharp sickle is told to gather the clusters of grapes from the earth, which are then thrown into the "great winepress of God's wrath" and trampled outside the city (14:19–20). Revelation 19:15 shows that Jesus himself "treads the winepress of the fury of the wrath of God Almighty." Both of these visions illustrate the fate of those who worship the beast (14:9–11):

> If anyone worships the beast and its image and receives its mark on their forehead or on their hand, they, too, will drink the wine of God's fury, which has been poured full strength into the cup of his wrath. They will be tormented with burning sulfur in the presence of the holy angels and of the Lamb. And the smoke of their torment will rise for ever and ever. There will be no rest day or night for those who worship the beast and its image, or for anyone who receives the mark of its name.

Revelation is not a politically correct, sentimental book, largely because it teaches the reality of a final judgment for the wicked. Gentle Jesus, meek and mild? Not always. He is not only the Savior; he is also the Judge. He's not only the Suffering Servant; he's also the Warrior Christ. He is the Lamb of God, who was slain for our sins, but also a Ram with seven horns and seven eyes, symbolic of his perfect strength and penetrating insight (5:6). The Lamb is also the Lord of lords and the King of kings (17:14). While it's tempting to create Jesus in our own image so that he's under our control, the biblical Jesus refuses to be tamed. While judgment is sometimes difficult to comprehend, what is even more dreadful is the thought that evil might never face justice, that evil might get away with evil. That's a truly horrifying thought.

In the center of the book, there are three sets of judgment visions, each with seven parts—the seven seals (6:1–17;

8:1), seven trumpets (8:7–9:21; 11:14–19), and seven bowls (16:1–21). (See the chart for a visual representation of how these judgments unfold.) Like the plagues God sent against the Egyptians when he delivered his people from captivity (Exodus 7–11), these three series provide the centerpiece of his judgment against evil in the book of Revelation. The judgments even resemble the Egyptian plagues at points. As we saw earlier, some of these visions relate to large periods of human history (especially the first four seals), and some relate to the very end of history. It's hard to know exactly how all this will play out in our world, but we can be certain about a few things.

First, notice how the judgments increase in intensity as you move from the seals to the bowls (from one-fourth to one-third to one). God is patient and slowly turns up the pressure on the wicked in hopes that they will turn back to him. There is mercy even as his judgment unfolds.

Second, there is an interlude between the sixth and seventh seal and trumpet judgments, but there is no interlude before the seventh bowl judgment, because the end of history is very close at hand. These interludes, or dramatic pauses, show us the current situation of God's people, including what they are being called to do and why they should not give up hope. Revelation's message for us often shows up best in these interludes.

Third, all three series arrive at the same place: the end of the age and God's judgment of the whole world. You see a storm-earthquake in 8:3–5; 11:19; and 16:18, which indicates the breaking up of creation and God's final judgment. When you get to the end of each series, you're at the very end of human history. So, to some extent these series repeat God's ongoing judgments of the wicked. Revelation spirals forward in repeated cycles of judgment rather than progressing in a neat, straight line. Perhaps this slow movement shows us God's patience. Peter says as much in one of his letters when explaining why Christ has not yet returned: "The Lord is not slow in keeping his promise, as some understand slowness. Instead he is patient

The Three Series of Judgments in Revelation

	Seals (6:1–17; 8:1)	Trumpets (8:7–9:21; 11:14–19)	Interlude—12:1–14:20	Bowls (16:1–21)
1	White horse—military conquest	Hail and fire, mixed with blood, burn up one-third of earth		Sores on those with beast's mark
2	Red horse—violent bloodshed	Burning mountain causes a third of sea to turn to blood and destroys a third of creatures and ships		Sea turns to blood and everything in it dies
3	Black horse—famine	Blazing star (Wormwood) turns a third of fresh water bitter, killing many		Rivers and springs turned to blood
4	Pale horse—death and Hades bring death to one-fourth of earth	A third of sun, moon, and stars turned dark		Sun scorches people with fire and they curse God
5	Martyrs cry out to God for vindication and are told to wait	Fallen star opens Abyss, releasing scorpion-locusts to harm those without seal of God for five months		Throne of beast cursed with darkness. Again, people in agony curse God
6	Shaking of entire cosmos followed by wicked attempting to hide from wrath of God and Lamb	Release of four angels bound at Euphrates, who then raise an army of serpent-lions to kill a third of people on earth		River Euphrates dried up as demonic forces gather kings of earth for battle at Armageddon
	Interlude—7:1–17	Interlude—10:1–11:13		No interlude
7	Silence and seven trumpets	Christ's kingdom arrives as elders thank God for his judgment, rewarding of saints, and vindication of his people		Voice from temple says, "It is done," followed by storm-quake and destruction of Babylon by God; islands and mountains disappear and huge hailstones fall on people, who respond by cursing God
	Storm-earthquake at 8:3–5	Storm-earthquake at 11:19		Storm-earthquake at 16:18

with you, not wanting anyone to perish, but everyone to come to repentance" (2 Pet 3:9).

The climactic vision of judgment in Revelation is the return of Christ in 19:11–21. He is seated on a white horse, reminiscent of a Roman general. With justice he judges and wages war. His eyes are like blazing fire, and on his head are many crowns. His robe is dipped in blood, and he leads the armies of heaven. His name is the Word of God, and out of his mouth comes a sharp sword to strike down the nations and rule them with an iron scepter. As the King of kings and Lord of lords, he treads the winepress of the fury of the wrath of God Almighty. Wow! What a description of the Warrior-Judge-King returning in all his glorious might to defeat his enemies and establish his universal reign! This doesn't sound like the same Jesus we read about in the Gospels, but we have to remember the context. Here in Revelation 19, Jesus is returning to destroy evil once and for all, and he doesn't tiptoe into spiritual battle with the forces of darkness.

As we've already seen, the famous battle of Armageddon that follows is anticlimactic—"the beast was captured" (19:20). Christ conquers simply by his appearance. He returns and judges his enemies by his word. Game over. The passage closes with God's enemies actually becoming a banquet for the birds of prey, a gruesome image that stands in contrast to the messianic wedding banquet of the Lamb. Finally, we come to the final judgment vision of Revelation 20.

The Final Judgment

Throughout Revelation a battle rages between the forces of evil, on the one hand, and God and his people, on the other. Finally, God has had enough, and we read of the final judgment in 20:7–15. After Satan is released from his temporary imprisonment during the Millennium, he gathers the wicked nations for a final battle (20:7–8). The army of the ungodly surrounds the camp of God's people. All hope seems lost as the enemy closes in. But just like the battle of Armageddon, there is no actual battle. When God decides to act, he wins! He sends fire from heaven to devour the evil army (20:9). Then we are told that God's archenemy, Satan, the master of deception, accusation, and death, is thrown into the fiery lake, where he joins the beast and false prophet (20:10). The unholy trinity will be tormented for eternity.

The great white throne judgment of 20:11–15 further explains the final judgment of the wicked mentioned in 20:9. I do think that Christians will one day give an account of how they have lived—at the judgment seat of Christ, where they will receive or forfeit rewards (2 Cor 5:10; cf. 1 Cor 3:10–15). But I don't think Christians will stand before God at the great white throne judgment of Revelation 20. God has already judged the eternal destiny of his people by virtue of their resurrection (19:14; 20:4–6). God would not raise a person from the dead, give him a brand-new resurrection body prepared for life in the new heaven and new earth, and then condemn him to hell. And this final judgment occurs after God's people have been resurrected.

The great white throne judgment is a destiny judgment for the unrighteous. The wicked are held accountable for their ungodly actions. These actions are confirmed by their names not being included in the "book of life" (13:8; 17:8; 20:12, 15), the heavenly register of all true believers—those who have been granted heavenly citizenship. Since wicked human beings have rejected Christ and rebelled against God, they will join the unholy trinity in the fiery lake.

The lake of fire, traditionally known as "hell" (Gk. *Gehenna*), is the place of final punishment. This is the "second death" since it represents eternal separation from the presence of God and anything connected to the life he gives. After evil powers and people have been thrown into the lake of fire, "death and Hades" are cast in as well. I once said to grieving people at a funeral that God will one day tell death to go to hell. It's true.

He will. Here we see the eternal death of death, the last enemy, which has caused so much pain and sorrow since Genesis 3 (21:4; 1 Cor 15:26). In the end, all of God's enemies suffer the same fiery fate—the beast and the false prophet (19:20), Satan (20:10), death (20:14), and wicked humans (20:15; 21:8).

In spite of our knowledge that God judges righteously and perfectly, the thought of unbelievers facing eternal judgment in hell is enormously sobering. Because the word "hell" is used carelessly in our society, and because the Bible's teaching on hell definitely cuts against the grain of popular beliefs, we can sometimes forget that hell is a real and serious consequence for real people, people we know. Francis Chan and Preston Sprinkle coauthored the book *Erasing Hell*, in which they argue for a biblical view of the place of final punishment. They remind us that this is not just a doctrinal discussion but also a very personal one:

> What causes my heart to ache right now as I'm writing this is that my life shows little evidence that I actually believe this. Every time my thoughts wander to the future of unbelievers, I quickly brush them aside so they don't ruin my day. But there is a reality here that I can't ignore. Even as the conversations of people around me fill my ears, the truth of Scripture penetrates my heart with sobering statements about their destinies. We can talk about the fate of some hypothetical person, but as I look up and see their smiles, I have to ask myself if I really believe what I have written in this book. Hell is for real. *Am I?*[7]

Dealing honestly with the biblical truth that God will judge the wicked brings us face-to-face with God's absolute holiness and purity and should motivate us to pray for and reach out to our unbelieving friends with the good news of Jesus Christ.

Conclusion

I know it must be hard to read about judgment. If it helps, judgment is not my favorite topic to write about either. But we live in a broken world where evil is real. How horrible it would be to live in a world with no justice, a world where evil wins. That would be much, much worse than thinking about judgment. We need a good and holy and powerful God who can and will judge evil.

Those who have suffered very little often just want God to be nice to everyone, while those who have experienced persecution or injustice cry out for God to set things right. And God promises to do just that. He will not sweep the abuse and violence and injustice you have experienced or witnessed under the cosmic rug and pretend it never happened. God is holy and righteous and will punish evil. On top of that, God will root out evil completely and totally. He will destroy Satan and sin and death. The new creation will not only be free from evil but also be free from all causes and agents of evil so that evil won't make a comeback in the future. There must be a total and absolute cleansing of creation, a death and resurrection, you might say.

As we think about judgment, it's important to remember God's heart. God is holy and righteous and pure and hates sin and evil, but his desire is for people to repent and return to him. He takes no delight in judging evildoers, but he cannot compromise his character. Revelation stresses God's patience. In speaking to the seven churches, Jesus calls his people to repent (2:5, 16, 22; 3:3, 19). He warns them to turn away from patterns of sin that include lovelessness, false teaching, immorality, idolatry, and spiritual lethargy, so they won't face judgment.

In the seal, trumpet, and bowl judgments, we move from one-fourth to one-third to one, showing the slow and progressive nature of these judgments—signs of God's patience. We repeatedly see unbelievers stubbornly refuse to give up their sins in spite of tasting God's judgment. In 9:20–21 we read:

> The rest of mankind who were not killed by these plagues still did not repent of the work of their hands; they did not stop worshiping demons, and idols of gold, silver, bronze, stone and

wood—idols that cannot see or hear or walk. Nor did they repent of their murders, their magic arts, their sexual immorality or their thefts.

Near the end of the bowl judgments, we read that the unbelievers "cursed the name of God" and "refused to repent" (16:9, 11, 21). Their hearts are hard, preferring to curse God rather than submit to him. In their rejection of God's offer of repentance, we see the great tragedy of human sin—that people pursue the very things that will destroy them. The core of sin and evil is rejecting God as the center and source of life and trying to live independently of God. C. S. Lewis reminds us that the people who will populate hell won't want to live in heaven: "There are only two kinds of people in the end: those who say to God, 'Thy will be done,' and those to whom God says in the end, '*Thy* will be done.' All that are in Hell, choose it."[8]

God's judgment is not something to be taken lightly. As the writer of Hebrews says, "It is a dreadful thing to fall into the hands of the living God" (Heb 10:31). I can't think of anything more terrifying. Revelation calls us to make sure we are part of God's covenant community and to persevere in our confession of Jesus as Lord. The beautiful thing about the good news of Jesus is that for those who are in Christ, the judgment has already occurred (Rom 8:1). In Christ, we have been completely forgiven; we have been fully accepted into God's covenant family; and we will never be condemned.

It's also crucial for us to have the right perspective on judgment. Judgment is God's role, not ours. Our job is to follow the Lord with our whole heart and not to set ourselves up as the world's judge. Judgment is God's business. We should pray for our enemies and love them in hopes that they will return to God (Matt 5:44–45; Rom 12:14, 17–20). We can praise God for judging evil and at the same time pray for and love unbelievers, hoping they will experience a relationship with Jesus.

God will judge evil. But judgment is not God's final word for his people or his creation. His final word takes us back to the first book of the Bible: "In the beginning God created the heavens and the earth" (Gen 1:1). Here in the final book of the Bible we see that God's last word is not judgment but creation: "Then I saw 'a new heaven and a new earth'" (21:1).

Key texts: Rev 9:20–21; 14:9–11; 16:12–21; 19:19–21; 20:7–15
Reading plan: Revelation 6; 8–9; 16; 20

Community Group Questions

1. What have you grown up believing about God's judgment? What is one way your beliefs have been changed by looking at the theme of judgment in Revelation?
2. How does God's wrath differ from human anger or wrath? Why does this difference matter?
3. How does God's character relate to judgment? Why is this so important?
4. What do you think about God's strategy of allowing evil to destroy itself?
5. Where did we get the idea that Armageddon was a real battle? How does Revelation change our understanding of God's defeat of evil in the end?
6. God seems to be taking his time about judging evil. Would you prefer that he judge evil instantly? What are some pros and cons of God's patient judgment of evil?
7. What helps us trust God as the Judge without trying to become judges ourselves? In other words, how can we keep God's role and our roles separate?

9

THE NEW CREATION

"I Saw 'a New Heaven and a New Earth'"

I grew up with a dreadfully boring, sterile, and unbiblical concept of heaven. When you die, you go to heaven, this place in the sky with winged angels, white cloudy smoke, and pearly gates, with Saint Peter either granting or denying permission to enter. Everyone is dressed in white and floating around not doing much of anything, with organ or harp music playing in the background. I'm a bit fuzzy on what happens after that. I've always been told that everyone will love heaven and you should want to go there, but I never really did, at least not to that sort of heaven. I remember sitting on a hard pew, singing a six-stanza hymn, hoping that the heaven we were singing about would turn out to be a lot more colorful, realistic, familiar, and relational than my paltry mental picture.

How tragic! The sermons I heard were usually about getting saved or rededicating your life or sharing the gospel or becoming a missionary or something similar, and almost never about heaven. I don't ever remember hearing a sermon on heaven. In all fairness to my church leaders, perhaps there were sermons on heaven, but the few I might have heard never made a lasting impression on me or made me want to go there. If you also have a lousy view of heaven, Revelation will change that.

Revelation doesn't say we go to heaven so much as heaven comes down to us from God . . . as a gift (21:2). Even better, Revelation doesn't just say "heaven" but speaks of "a new heaven *and* a new earth" (21:1), meaning a whole new world, much like the one we live in now but perfectly better. Just as Christians will one day be raised from the dead and given new resurrection bodies, so this fallen world will also be re-created—a new earth and a new sky, a whole new world. As you read about the new creation God has in store for his people, prepare to be pleasantly surprised. My hope is that after hearing what Revelation says about the new creation you will actually want to go there—perhaps not at this very moment, but in God's time.

Promise

A promise is only as good as its maker, and our God has made us some pretty big promises about what is to come. As you have read what Jesus promised the victors in Revelation 2–3, perhaps you noticed that almost all of the promises relate to the future. The victors are guaranteed eternal life (2:7); deliverance from eternal punishment (2:11); acceptance, care, and provision (2:17); a share in Jesus's authority (2:26–28; 3:21); a secure and permanent citizenship in the heavenly city (3:4–5); and life forever in God's presence (3:12). For people who were under constant threat from things like starvation, disease, earthquakes, false religion, and pagan political powers, these promises carried a lot of weight. Promises of a better future always bring hope to people who are struggling.

These specific promises are part of God's much bigger promise that touches the whole story of the Bible.[1] From the time Adam and Eve sinned, God has been working to restore fellowship with his creation. The triune God is the perfect community,

160

and nothing will derail his plan to share his relational goodness with his people in a restored creation. God's promise to one day live among his people goes back a long time. The Old Testament repeats this promise many times, often with three parts (e.g., Lev 26:12; Jer 31:33; Ezek 37:27; cf. 2 Cor 6:16):

- I will be your God.
- You will be my people.
- I will live among you.

God doesn't just promise that we will go to heaven when we die. It's much, much bigger than that. Since our fall into sin, God has been working to restore everything, to fix everything, all with the goal of living among his people in perfect community. That's why he made the covenant with Abraham and why he delivered the people from slavery in Egypt and why he gave instructions for the tabernacle, and later the temple. That's why Jesus came to earth to minister and die on the cross and be raised from the dead. That's why the Spirit came to indwell us and why we're taking the good news to the nations. What God began early in Genesis, he now finishes late in Revelation. Take a look at how wide ranging and all-embracing God's promise really is in the chart below that compares the first few chapters of Genesis with the last few chapters of Revelation. The first thing to see about the new creation is that it's the fulfillment of God's promise, and God always keeps his promises.

Place

I grew up in one house in a small town in Texas. Life happened in that place. Whether it was playing football in the yard or basketball in the driveway, working in the garage, enjoying a wonderful meal in the kitchen, watching a movie in the living room, or sleeping late in the bedroom—I cannot separate my childhood from that place. My parents are now with the Lord,

Genesis and Revelation

Genesis	The Beginning	The End	Revelation
1:1	"In the beginning God . . ."	"I am the Alpha and the Omega, the Beginning and the End."	21:6
1:1	God creates first heaven and earth, eventually cursed by sin.	God creates a new heaven and earth, where sin is nowhere to be found.	21:1
1:2	Water symbolizes unordered chaos.	There is no longer any sea.	21:1
1:3–5	God creates light and separates it from darkness.	There is no more night or natural light; God himself is the source of light.	21:23; 22:5
1:26–30	God gives humans dominion over the earth.	God's people will reign with him forever.	20:4, 6; 22:5
1:27–28; 2:7, 18–25	"Marriage" of Adam and Eve	Marriage of the Last Adam and his bride, the church	19:7; 21:2, 9
3:1–7	Satan introduces sin into the world.	Satan and sin are judged.	19:11–21; 20:7–10
3:1–7, 13–15	The serpent deceives humanity.	The ancient serpent is bound, "to keep him from deceiving the nations."	20:2–3
3:3; 4:6–8; 6:3	Death enters the world.	Death is put to death.	20:14; 21:4
3:6	Sin enters the world.	Sin is banished from God's city.	21:8, 27; 22:15
3:6–7; 4:6–8; 6:5	Sinful people refuse to serve/obey God.	God's people serve him.	22:3
3:8; 4:8	Community is forfeited.	Genuine community is experienced.	21:3, 7
3:8–10; 6:5	God is abandoned by sinful people.	God's people (new Jerusalem, bride of Christ) are made ready for God and the marriage of the Lamb.	19:7–8; 21:2, 9–21
3:8–11	Sinful people are ashamed in God's presence.	God's people will "see his face."	22:4
3:8–19	People rebel against the true God, resulting in physical and spiritual death.	God's people risk death to worship the true God and thus experience life.	20:4–6

162

The New Creation

Genesis	The Beginning	The End	Revelation
3:16–17; 6:5–6	Sin brings pain and tears.	God comforts his people and removes crying and pain.	21:4
3:16–19	Sinful people are cursed.	The curse is removed from redeemed humanity, and they become a blessing.	22:3
3:22–24	Sinful people are forbidden to eat from the tree of life.	God's people may eat freely from the tree of life.	22:2, 14
3:22–24	Sinful people are sent away from life.	God's people have their names written in the book of life.	20:4–6, 15; 21:6, 27
3:23	Exclusion from the bounty of Eden	Invitation to the marriage supper of the Lamb	19:9
3:23–24	Sinful humanity is separated from the presence of the holy God.	God's people experience God's holiness (cubed city = Most Holy Place).	21:15–21
3:23–24	Sinful people are sent away from the garden.	New heaven/earth includes a garden.	22:2
3:24	Sinful people are banished from the presence of God.	God lives among his people.	21:3, 7, 22; 22:4
4:10–14	Sinful humanity is cursed with wandering (exile).	God's people are given a permanent home.	21:3
4:11–14	Sinful humanity suffers a wandering exile.	God gives his children an inheritance.	21:7
5:6, 8, 14, 17, 20, 27, 31; 6:3	Creation begins to grow old and die.	All things are made new.	21:5
6:5	Sin results in spiritual sickness.	God heals the nations.	22:2
6:1–7:24	Water is used to destroy wicked humanity.	God quenches thirst with water from the spring of life.	21:6; 22:1
11:3–9	Sinful people are scattered.	God's people unite to sing his praises.	19:6–7
11:8–9	Languages of sinful humanity are confused.	God's people are a multicultural people.	21:24, 26; 22:2

163

but I occasionally drive by the house, and I'm always hit with a strong wave of nostalgia. I have a deep emotional attachment to that particular place and always will.

I think place is the most underrated aspect of life. To say it another way, place is much, much more significant than we sometimes think, and it's sad that we often fail to appreciate its influence and power. Life itself, good or bad, is connected to important places. We are place people. Right now, I'm sitting on our long, shaded front porch on a beautiful autumn morning expressing my thoughts in writing. I love this place.

Our love of place comes from the God of place. Our relationship with God isn't just mental or imaginary or "spiritual"; it happens in a physical, flesh-and-blood place. The new creation will be such a place. We need to throw out the idea that one day we'll float up into the sky and live forever as disembodied souls in God's mystical presence. Again, it's a new heaven (or sky) *and* a new earth (or land). The present world will be totally transformed into a new world, just as our present bodies will be totally transformed through resurrection into new bodies fit for life in a whole new place.

John says in 21:1: "Then I saw 'a new heaven and a new earth,' for the first heaven and the first earth had passed away, and there was no longer any sea." In 21:2 he sees "the Holy City, the new Jerusalem, coming down out of heaven from God, prepared as a bride beautifully dressed for her husband" (cf. 3:12). In 21:5, for the first time since 1:8 God himself speaks directly: "I am making everything new!"

As you read Revelation 21–22, you'll notice that this whole new world is both a garden and a city. By "garden" the Bible doesn't mean a small flower garden in someone's backyard, but it is referring to more like a national park covering hundreds of thousands of acres of mountains and lakes and prairies and magnificent waterfalls and flower-carpeted meadows. The whole world will be a garden, a place of unimaginable beauty.

When I think of natural beauty, I think of *National Geographic* pictures of the Swiss Alps, the Hawaiian Islands, the wheat fields of Kansas, the Smoky Mountains, the Grand Canyon, the great botanical gardens, striking sunsets, majestic rivers, and so on. If you like the beauty of this world, you're going to love the new world God has planned. Why would the new creation be less beautiful, less breathtaking, less amazing than this world? It won't! God created this world, and he wouldn't save the worst for last. If you like this world, you're going to love the new creation! God invented beauty, and our most beautiful experiences now are only hints of the beauty that awaits us in the eternal garden city of the new heaven and new earth.

The new heaven and new earth are hard to imagine because we only have samples and glimpses and hints of the variety, color, goodness, and glory that awaits us there. That's exactly why the Bible so often describes the new world in terms of what it does *not* include. Revelation uses expressions such as "never again" or "no more" to assure us that the new creation will not include any of the bad stuff:

> Therefore,
> "they are before the throne of God
>   and serve him day and night in his temple;
> and he who sits on the throne
>   will shelter them with his presence.
> 'Never again will they hunger;
>   never again will they thirst.
> The sun will not beat down on them,'
>   nor any scorching heat.
> For the Lamb at the center of the throne
>   will be their shepherd;
> 'he will lead them to springs of living water.'
>   'And God will wipe away every tear from their eyes.'"
> (7:15–17)

And I heard a loud voice from the throne saying, "Look! God's dwelling place is now among the people, and he will dwell with them. They will be his people, and God himself will be with them and be their God. 'He will wipe every tear from their eyes. There will be no more death' or mourning or crying or pain, for the old order of things has passed away." He who was seated on the throne said, "I am making everything new!" Then he said, "Write this down, for these words are trustworthy and true." (21:3–5)

There will be no more night or darkness in heaven, only light (21:23, 25; 22:5). There will be no more hunger or thirst or scorching heat (7:16). Instead, we may eat freely from the tree of life (2:7; 22:14) and drink freely of the water of life (7:17; 21:6; 22:1, 17). No more curse (22:3–5). No more disease (22:2, 14, 19). No more crying or pain or mourning or death (7:17; 21:4). All that is sinful will be completely banned from heaven (21:4–5, 7–8; 22:3, 14–15). God himself will wipe away all our tears (7:17; 21:4). All life, no death (2:10–11). The new creation is not a massive undoing of what God has done here but rather the great transformation of his first creation.

Don't we long for a place without any danger or disease or death, a place where evil is totally absent? All we will know in that resurrected place is security, provision, peace, and joy, all because we will be living in the very presence of our life-giving God.

People

The new creation isn't just a place; it's also a people. Revelation speaks to us about where God's people come from, who we are as his people, and what we are supposed to do. To begin with, John tells us several times that God's people will come from all over the world: "After this I looked, and there before me was a great multitude that no one could count, from every nation, tribe, people and language, standing before the throne and before the Lamb" (7:9; also 19:1–3, 6–8). This great multitude has been purchased for God by Christ (5:9) so that God is rightly praised as the "King of the nations," as people from all nations will come and worship the Lord (15:3–4). Just as the new creation will be a multicolored place, so we should expect it to be populated by a multiethnic people. Living in the new heaven and new earth will not erase our differences but instead perfect them.

When describing the heavenly city, John says that "the glory and honor of the nations" will be brought into this new Jerusalem (21:24, 26). Since 21:27 makes it clear that nothing ungodly can enter the city, including the wicked nations who earlier rebelled against God (e.g., 20:8–10), the "glory and honor of the nations" must refer to the redeemed from among the various nations. This fulfills the Old Testament expectation of the day when redeemed Gentiles would live among God's people in the heavenly city (e.g., Zech 2:11).

As we saw earlier, when John describes the tree of life in Revelation 22, he borrows from Ezekiel 47 with only one slight but significant change:

Ezekiel 47:12: "Their fruit will serve for food and their leaves for healing."

Revelation 22:2: "And the leaves of the tree are for the healing *of the nations*."

The new creation provides ultimate healing for God's multicultural people redeemed from all over the world. This has always been God's plan, as God told Abraham when he first called him: "All peoples on earth will be blessed through you" (Gen 12:3). Think about how amazing it will be to spend forever meeting different people and exploring different cultures as we join together to worship the Lord!

A second important question relates to our identity. Who are we as the people of God? God's people are identified as pure, devoted, truthful, faithful, and blameless. God's people are, in a word, godly. In Rev 14:4–5, they are portrayed as ethical virgins who refuse to compromise with the world but instead "follow the Lamb wherever he goes." To the faithful in Sardis, Jesus promises they will one day walk with him, "dressed in white, for they are worthy" (3:4–5). In 6:11, the martyrs are given a white robe and told to wait a little longer for God's justice. The great multitude standing before the throne in 7:9 is wearing white robes and holding palm branches. They have come through the great tribulation and (paradoxically) have washed their robes white in the red blood of the Lamb (7:13–14). White clothing often symbolizes purity and victory through tribulation, all made possible by the sacrificial death of Christ (see 12:11). We are told in 19:8 that the fine linen worn by believers "stands for the righteous acts of God's holy people." All this is to emphasize the righteous character of God's new-creation people. Nothing impure or shameful or deceitful will enter the heavenly city (21:27).

Our identity doesn't just consist of our righteous behavior; it's also much more personal, even intimate. We are God's children destined to receive an inheritance: "Those who are victorious will inherit all this, and I will be their God and they will be my children" (21:7). God sometimes calls John to mix his images in order to communicate another important part of our identity, and he does so here. The children are also the bride (19:7–8): "Let us rejoice and be glad and give him glory! For the wedding of the Lamb has come, and his bride has made herself ready. Fine linen, bright and clean, was given her to wear."

Throughout Scripture, the marriage image depicts the identity of God's people like no other. The Old Testament prophets even speak of Israel as Yahweh's wife or, when rebellious, as an adulteress (see Hos 2:1–23 for both). The New Testament speaks of Jesus as the Bridegroom (Mark 2:19–20; John 3:29) and the church as his bride (2 Cor 11:2; Eph 5:25–33; Rev

19:7; 21:2, 9; 22:17). Such marriage talk leaves us knowing deep down that God loves us perfectly and invites us to look forward to experiencing his personal presence in the new creation. It also assures us that one day we will be completely dedicated to the one true God and no longer be tempted to chase after other gods.

To mix the images even more, the bride is also a building or a temple, the very place where God lives for eternity. In John's vision of the new heaven and new earth in Revelation 21, he specifically sees the "Holy City, the new Jerusalem, coming down out of heaven from God, prepared as a bride beautifully dressed for her husband" (21:2). In other parts of the New Testament, the church is portrayed as the temple of God's Spirit (1 Cor 3:16–17; 2 Cor 6:16; Eph 2:21–22; 1 Pet 2:5). The heavenly city doesn't need a separate temple since the entire new creation has become God's dwelling place, or temple (Rev 21:22). The logic can be confusing—children, garden city, bride, temple—but this is picture language, and it's perfectly fine to mix metaphors. In a sense, it's more important that we're overwhelmed with the goodness and richness of the images as we try to absorb and experience each one than that we try to map them all out in a logical format.

Back to identity. Revelation assures us that our identity is secure. You might say that God's name has been stamped on us (3:12; 14:1; 22:4). We're like pillars or permanent fixtures in God's heavenly temple (3:12). Such security meant a lot to the first readers, who were often kicked out of the synagogue or excluded from the local trade guild for their commitment to Christ. It also means a lot to many of us who have experienced opposition or rejection because we've stood firm for Christ. It does raise an important spiritual question for each of us: Where does our security lie?

Finally, Revelation speaks to us about what God's people are supposed to do. If the new creation is a perfect place, and a place of rest at that, will there be anything to do in heaven?

How can you improve upon perfection? Does heaven mean no play, no work, no activity, only rest? Will we be bored forever?

Revelation makes it clear that we will have plenty to do for eternity. To begin with, heavenly rest will mean a permanent break from all the stress, chaos, shattered relationships, and spiritual battles of this broken world, but it won't mean inactivity (14:13). We rest not by doing nothing but by doing the things we love, things in line with God's creative, life-giving character. We will finally get relief from our struggle against Satan and sin, but we will never be bored. There will be plenty to do, and we will enjoy every minute of it.

What exactly will we be doing? For starters, we will worship and serve God: "They are before the throne of God and serve him day and night in his temple" (7:15), and "the throne of God and of the Lamb will be in the city, and his servants will serve him" (22:3). The term for "serve" (Gk. *latreuō*) implies the kind of service that is worshipful through and through. The new creation will be a place always on fire with worship (see 4:8–11; 5:6–14; 7:9–17; 15:2–3; 19:1–8).

According to Revelation, singing will play a huge role in our heavenly worship. The angelic beings are full of song (4:8; 5:8). Believers also join in this heavenly anthem of praise to God (7:9–10). I guess you could say that the angels will teach us how to sing. It's fascinating that the 144,000 (symbolic of the whole people of God) will sing "a new song before the throne" and "no one could learn the song except the 144,000 who had been redeemed from the earth" (14:3). Like other "new songs" in Scripture, such as the one Moses sang in Exodus 15 after God delivered his people from slavery in Egypt, this one will also celebrate God's mighty acts of victory over his enemies (e.g., Isa 42:10–13). The scene is repeated with more detail in 15:2–4, where the victorious heavenly multitude holds harps given to them by God and sing "the song of God's servant Moses and of the Lamb."

Recently, my wife and I were facing a seemingly impossible family situation, and I told her, "I feel like the Egyptian army is on our heels and God hasn't yet opened up the sea." After our ordeal had passed, we praised God with a depth of relief that we don't experience every day. God's triumph over Pharaoh and his army in the exodus event points forward to his final triumph over Satan and the demonic army. We will one day sing that song of victorious relief that Moses once sang (Exod 15:1–18). Ultimately, the song of Moses is also the song of the Lamb, one song celebrating the deliverance God has given to his people.

In the new creation, we will do more than worship. Many times in Revelation we are also told, as surprising as it may seem, that we will reign or rule with the Lord (2:26–27; 3:21; 5:10; 20:4–6; 22:5):

You have made them to be a kingdom and priests to serve our God, and they will reign on the earth. (5:10)

There will be no more night. They will not need the light of a lamp or the light of the sun, for the Lord God will give them light. And they will reign for ever and ever. (22:5)

Rule or reign with Christ over what? Probably over the new creation itself. I wonder if C. S. Lewis had been reading Revelation when he decided to make Peter and Susan and Edmund and Lucy kings and queens in Narnia. They rule over Narnia, and one day we will rule with Christ over the new creation.

The new creation won't be one eternally exhausting church service, but neither will it be an endless vacation. Just as Adam and Eve were entrusted with ruling in the original garden (Gen 1:26, 28), so God's people will also bear the responsibility of reigning with him in the eternal garden city. We will get it right this time around. Work is good and was part of God's original creation before sin entered the picture. We will definitely do things in heaven. You could call it work, but it will be full of meaning and purpose. No frustration, no waste. It might feel a lot more like play than work. The new heaven and new earth will be not the absence of responsibility but the fulfillment of our God-given purpose. We won't be bored. Instead, we will be totally absorbed with significant activity that pleases the Lord. Since God is infinite, we will never exhaust him or his new creation, even though we will be learning and growing, serving and reigning and worshiping forever.[2]

Presence

I'm convinced that the main reason God created us was for us to love him and live in his presence forever. God has always wanted to live among his people, a people who would freely and wholeheartedly respond to his love by loving him in return. He created us to enjoy the perfect community—fellowship with the triune God. As we saw in chapter 1, the Bible is really a story about God working out his plan to transform and live among his people. As you read the Old Testament, you'll notice that God lived among his people by means of a tabernacle and later a temple, yet he promised to one day do so in a more personal and permanent way. Again, his three-part promise can be summarized like this: "I will be your God, you will be my people, and I will live among you" (e.g., Exod 29:45–46; Lev 26:11–12; Jer 32:38; Ezek 37:27; Zech 2:10–11).

The New Testament begins with Jesus coming to earth to "tabernacle," or live, among us (see John 1:14). He later sent the Holy Spirit to live within individual believers, making the people of God the temple of God's Spirit (see 1 Cor 3:16–17; 6:19; 2 Cor 6:16; Eph 2:21–22; Heb 3:6; 1 Pet 2:4–5). But God wants to do more than to occupy a building among us or walk among us or even live within and among us. He wants us to live with him in a whole new world. We are told that there will be no physical temple in this new creation "because the Lord

God Almighty and the Lamb are its temple" (Rev 21:22). The heavenly city itself will be a cube, the very shape of the Most Holy Place in the ancient temple (see 1 Kgs 6:20; 2 Chr 3:8–9). Just as God's presence once lived in the Most Holy Place, so his presence will one day permeate the entire new heaven and new earth (Rev 21:15–17, 22). In other words, the whole new creation will become a Most Holy Place. As we get to the end of the grand story of Scripture, we see that God has kept his promise to live among his people. Revelation 21–22 gives us a breathtaking and hopeful preview of what it will be like to enjoy God's presence forever.

According to Revelation, living in God's very presence will bring new realities. First, God will be the recognized center of everything. When God's kingdom has fully and finally come with the new creation, the throne of God and the Lamb will sit at its center. Everything will revolve around God's powerful and personal presence symbolized by his throne (4:2; 5:1; 7:9; 21:3, 5). We read in 22:1 that the river of the water of life will flow from the throne of God and the Lamb into the whole of the new creation. Right now, we live with confusion and doubt and limited access to God. Using the apostle Paul's metaphor, it's as if we're trying to see life through a reflection in a dull mirror. But one day "we shall see face to face" (1 Cor 13:12). Now we know only in part, but then we shall know fully, even as we are fully known now. We live by faith in a strange and dangerous land. But then, the entire new universe will recognize God and the Lamb and the Spirit as the epicenter of all reality. No second-guessing, no uncertainty, no insecurity.

Second, we will experience God's presence in ways that we can't even imagine now. Revelation tells us that once we are in God's presence, he will "wipe every tear" from our eyes (21:4) and we will "see his face" (22:4). Scripture sometimes speaks of God in human terms to help us understand him and his actions better. In other words, Scripture speaks our language when it talks about God's hands and face. The thought of God's hand wiping away our tears shows us God's tenderness and compassion. The idea of seeing God's face means we will have a clear and true understanding of who he is and be rightly related to him. Rather than cowering in fear, we will experience God's gentle comfort and perfect protection. We will know him as a beloved child knows a loving parent.

Third, God's presence will mean that all things will be as they should be. The kingdom of this world will have become the kingdom of our God, and he will reign forever and ever (11:15–16). Shalom will descend over God's creation: "The webbing together of God, humans, and all creation in justice, fulfillment, and delight is what the Hebrew prophets call *shalom*. . . . In the Bible, shalom means *universal flourishing, wholeness, and delight*. . . . Shalom, in other words, is the way things ought to be."[3] The presence of perfect shalom will also ensure the absence of all that is evil and disruptive to shalom: tears, death, mourning, crying, pain, and things like these (7:17; cf. Isa 25:8). In the new creation we won't experience anything that runs counter to God's character!

Fourth, living in God's presence will mean complete safety. We will be protected or sheltered: "And he who sits on the throne will shelter them with his presence" (7:15). When it says that God's presence will "shelter" or "tabernacle over" his people (cf. John 1:14), this recalls God's protection and guidance of his people during their wilderness journey after the exodus as he covered them with his Shekinah, his glorious and radiant presence (e.g., Exod 13:21–22; Isa 4:5–6). In the new creation, there will be no one to violate you or harm you. There will be nothing to endanger your life. You will be totally and completely safe.

Fifth, life in God's presence will be an experience of indescribable and glorious beauty. My family took a trip to Switzerland once. I can't really put into words how beautiful that place is—the majestic Alps, the lush meadows, the gorgeous flowers, beautiful homes and old church buildings . . . even the cows are beautiful in Switzerland. It was a postcard experience. Beauty has a mysterious way of healing our souls. Whether it is the innocence of one of our granddaughters or the radiance of a bride or a picturesque sunset or a walk in the stillness of a light snowfall, beauty brings depth and richness to life. Revelation reminds us in various ways that God invented beauty and has planned a beautiful new creation to come.

The eternal garden city is introduced in Rev 21:1–8, and that short description is then expanded in 21:9–22:5, where it is described as a holy city, a temple city, and a garden city. The new creation radiates God's glorious presence and displays his beauty. It's everything we would expect and more than we can imagine. The precious building materials, such as gold, and the brilliant jewels that adorn the city convey the new creation's beauty. God created beauty as much for us as for himself. He first assessed his own handiwork as "good" in Genesis 1, meaning not only that God saw that it was good work but also that it was good for us, his beloved creatures.

Finally, life in God's presence will be a party. Of all the ways God could have described his people entering into the new creation, he chose to describe it as a wedding celebration. You have a bride (21:2, 9) and a wedding supper (19:9) and all the joy that goes with it. Weddings are festive affairs, full of laughter, tears of joy, plenty of hugs, and a good supply of sumptuous food and drink. First-century Jewish weddings were generally better celebrations than our two-hour operations, largely because they lasted up to a week. Imagine how wonderful the heavenly celebration will be that lasts for eternity.

Conclusion

Revelation paints a picture of the new heaven and new earth that makes us want to go there. If you can imagine a place that looks like the most beautiful parts of our present world, a place where there is no sin or Satan or disease or death ("no more . . ."), a place where everyone loves the Lord and loves each other, and, most important, a place where the One who gave us life and gave his life for us will live among us—if you can even begin to imagine such a place, a place breathing in and breathing out pure life, then you are well on your way to imagining the biblical heaven.

The new creation will be the fulfillment of God's promise to live among us. This idea can be a bit scary until you let it sink in that every good thing that exists in our lives now comes from the Lord. He is our loving Father, who only wants to give us good things. He wants to be with us and wants us to be with him and to experience the perfect community, the very reality we were created for. In fact, all of our longings and desires for life and goodness and beauty will be completely fulfilled in the new creation because we will be dwelling in God's presence. We long for many good things now and catch glimpses of eternal joy through good books and music and road trips and friends and teammates and worship experiences and family and late-night talks and food and . . . Haven't you ever wanted a short time of such peace and joy and love to last forever because it was so wonderful, almost a fleeting glimpse of heaven? We long for that world, and that longing comes from God, and he intends to fulfill those longings and desires. He will keep his promises.

In the new creation God will assemble his multiethnic people from among the nations, people who have been redeemed by the blood of the Lamb. God's children and Christ's bride and the Spirit's temple will gather to sing praises to our God and reign with Christ over this new creation. We will have an eternity of meaningful work to do. We will live in shalom, where everything is as it should be. Complete safety. Glorious beauty. Eternal celebration. All this will be possible because we will live in the very Shekinah presence of God.

I encourage you to think about this new heaven and new earth to come. Let it saturate your mind and flood your imagination. C. S. Lewis once said, "If you read history you will find that the Christians who did most for the present world were just those who thought most of the next. . . . It is since Christians have largely ceased to think of the other world that they have become so ineffective in this."[4] It's true that "where there is life, there is hope," but it is also true that "where there is hope, there is life." Thinking of the new creation brings hope. Allowing ourselves to be transported in our imaginations to what God has planned for us often gives us strength to walk faithfully through this broken world as we long for things to be as they should be.

Key texts: Rev 7:15–17; 21:1–7, 22; 22:1–5
Reading plan: Revelation 21–22

Community Group Questions

1. What has been your primary understanding of heaven up to this point in your life? What, if anything, has always bothered you about the vision of heaven handed down to you?

2. Where do you think we get our traditional understanding of heaven, if not the Bible?

3. Revelation emphasizes the new creation as the fulfillment of a promise, a place, a people, and God's presence. Which of these means the most to you?

4. What has surprised you about Revelation's portrayal of the new creation?

5. Why do you suppose that the idea of living in God's presence makes many faithful Christians uncomfortable? What can be done to correct this idea?

6. Having read what Revelation says about the new creation, what are you most looking forward to?

7. How can a biblical understanding of the new creation strengthen your hope now like almost nothing else?

10

PERSEVERANCE

"To the One Who Is Victorious"

Have you ever thought much about what you really expect from the Christian life? When Judy and I had been married only a short time, an older, wiser person gave us some advice about expectations: you have to meet them or change them, or there will be conflict. Two options: meet expectations or change them. That wisdom has served us well over the years, and it doesn't apply just to marriage; it applies to all of life.

In the contemporary American church, the general expectation is that God has promised to make our lives safe and comfortable and happy. Our job is to follow him faithfully. We may not use these exact words to describe our expectations, but deep down most of us think the Christian life should run in this direction: if we follow God, he will protect us from harm and make our lives happier and easier. In our society, we enjoy many blessings of religious liberty: speaking freely about our faith, joining in Christian community without fear of persecution, teaching our children about Christ openly, wearing Christian symbols, having Christian books, and praying or reading the Bible in public. We don't think about being attacked physically because we are Christians, and the church continues to be a powerful public voice in our culture.

Unfortunately, many believers worldwide don't share our circumstances. They are persecuted and sometimes put to death for following Jesus.[1] The book of Revelation suggests that Christians should expect to suffer as a normal part of following Jesus. In Revelation, we hear a clear echo of the words of our Lord himself when he told his disciples, "In this world you will have trouble [*thlipsis*—common word for "tribulation" or "trial"]. But take heart! I have overcome the world" (John 16:33). It's interesting that when Jesus says he has "overcome" the world, he uses the same Greek word (*nikaō*) that is used throughout Revelation to call believers to win the victory over evil by persevering in faithfulness to God (e.g., 2:7, 11, 17, 26; 3:5, 12, 21). We desperately need to allow Revelation to adjust our expectations. Although comfort and happiness are wonderful, much of our world opposes our Lord and his ways. As a result, it makes perfect sense that if we remain faithful, the world that hated Jesus might not like us very much. Many of us need to change our expectations to include a willingness to suffer as we seek to stay faithful to Christ in the midst of a pagan world.

You might be wondering why the new creation is the next-to-the-last rather than the last chapter. I opted to put perseverance last because that brings us face-to-face with our main responsibility. Revelation isn't just about the future; it's also about how we live in the present. Even when we know the beautiful hope that lies ahead, we still need to endure. Perseverance is our primary task as we look forward to what God has in store. We are called to "follow the Lamb wherever he goes" (14:4). In this chapter, you'll learn that we really are in a war, a spiritual battle that sometimes results in the persecution and martyrdom of Christians. But we also need to remember the rewards that Jesus has promised to those who persevere.

We're in a War

Revelation suggests that Christians are in a real spiritual battle on two different fronts. First, we face opposition from a pagan world, resulting in persecution and, for some believers, even martyrdom. But the second aspect to the battle is equally dangerous and the one most of us will fight the majority of the time: the temptation to compromise with this same world system. While Revelation comforts those who are staying faithful (and suffering as a result), the book sternly warns those who are compromising. The war on two fronts comes down to this: opposition and temptation. Both are threats, and both test our resolve to persevere.

While some scholars have doubted that the Christians who first received the book of Revelation were actually facing persecution, the evidence in the book definitely points to at least some persecution, with the real possibility that things were about to get much worse. The messages to the seven churches mention persecution several times: endurance of hardships (2:3), slander (2:9), and imprisonment (2:10); the coming persecution (2:10); living in a difficult environment (2:13; 3:9); and the death of Antipas (2:13).

There are also references to persecution (or at least impending persecution) throughout the rest of the book. We read about those "who have come out of [i.e., endured through and have come out on the other side of] the great tribulation" in 7:13–14. The message of the little scroll in 10:9–11 is sour, likely referring to the coming suffering for God's people. The two witnesses of chapter 11, symbolic of the witnessing church, are put to death by the beast. We are called to triumph over the devil in 12:11 by our willingness to persevere unto death. There are multiple references to powers of this world shedding the blood of God's people (16:5–7; 17:6; 18:24; 19:2). Some Christians have been put to death because of their testimony about Jesus (20:4–6). In addition, there are important general statements throughout the book that describe a battle context: 12:12–17; 13:7; 14:13; 17:12–14.

Revelation demonstrates the truth of the apostle Paul's message to Timothy: "Everyone who wants to live a godly life in Christ Jesus will be persecuted" (2 Tim 3:12). This also introduces an important qualification. Not every Christian will actually be persecuted; only those who want to live a godly life in Christ. We can actually avoid persecution by staying in the background and not taking a stand, as did the majority of Christians in Germany during the Nazi takeover—the silent majority who did nothing to stop the Nazis. We can stay safe if we stay on the sidelines. But if we decide to live righteously, to stand for truth, to fight for justice, to speak out for the abused and mistreated, to make disciples, and to stay loyal to Christ and his kingdom no matter what, and to do so publicly, then we will most likely face opposition. We pray for wisdom to know when and how to take a stand, and for the courage to do so.

The most dangerous aspect of the battle for most of us, however, is not the threat of persecution but the temptation to compromise. The constant pressure to fit into the surrounding culture is powerful and shows up in several of the churches of Revelation: Ephesus has forsaken its first love (2:4), some at Pergamum and Thyatira are following false teachers (2:14–15, 20), Sardis has a reputation for being alive but is really dead (3:1), and Laodicea remains lukewarm (3:16–17). Let me explain a bit more about why they felt this pressure.

Life in the Roman Empire was built around devotion to the emperor, a system often referred to as the imperial cult. Such devotion pulled together political, social, economic, and military influences into a single dominating religious force, complete with temples, priests, festivals, and the like. The worship of the emperor often involved idolatrous and immoral activities (often associated with the local trade guilds) that would deeply offend Christians (e.g., having to confess that Caesar is Lord or joining in some sexual celebration in worship of a pagan deity). When Christians refused to participate, they would face the consequences. In addition, when you have false teachers within the church telling you that you can be a committed Christian and join in the immoral and idolatrous imperial cult activities at the same time (see 2:6, 14–15, 20–24), you understand how it is that many Christians would cave in to the pressure. But in the seven messages of Revelation 2–3, Jesus is very hard on those who compromise with the world system as well as those who encourage others to do the same.

The temptation to compromise with the pagan world isn't just a first-century problem. Today's world also tries to squeeze us into its mold. I've just lived through another Black Friday and Cyber Monday shopping frenzy connected to the Christmas season, and Christians seem just as caught up in the materialism and consumerism as non-Christians. Money seems to drive just about everything these days. We also feel the pressure to water down biblical truth in order to conform to the prevailing view on particular ethical issues. Movies and music often influence our thinking more than the Bible. The lure of power tempts us to lies and deception and cover-up. The enticement of pornography abounds. The temptation to compromise is alive and well today. We're in a real spiritual war, and the threat can be summed up in two words: immorality and idolatry.

Endure to the End

Using different words and images, Revelation tells us to be faithful to Jesus and to stay faithful until the end. The key factor here is time. We have to keep on trusting and keep on following until the end of our lives or until Jesus returns. We are called to be overcomers, or victors. As we have seen before, the term for "overcome" (Gk. *nikaō*, meaning "to win the victory") appears throughout Revelation to encourage Christians to persevere and endure in faithfulness. This is what Jesus himself did, and we are to follow his example. He was and is the Victorious One who triumphed at the cross and resurrection (3:21; 5:5) and will continue that triumph at his return (17:14). At the conclusion of each of the seven messages, Jesus makes promises to the victors (2:7, 11, 17, 26; 3:5, 12, 21). They win the victory by saying no to evil and saying yes to God and by staying faithful to the end.

Revelation 12:11 explains in a nutshell how we overcome: "They *triumphed* [that *nikaō* word again] over him by the blood of the Lamb and by the word of their testimony; they did not love their lives so much as to shrink from death." We rely on the victory that Christ has already won for us ("blood of the Lamb"), and we remain loyal to him even in the face of suffering and death. To be victorious or overcome in God's kingdom means "to follow the Lamb with one's whole life until the very end of one's life."[2] We are told at the end of the book that there are multitudes of people who will overcome (15:2; 21:7).

How Revelation tells us to overcome can be confusing for those of us who live in extremely competitive cultures where winning is defined as taking the initiative and moving forward and defeating our opponents. But in God's kingdom, he fights for us. He defeats our enemies. Our main task is to endure, to stand, to persevere, to stay the course, to remain faithful, to keep following the Lord. In the apostle Paul's teaching on spiritual warfare in Ephesians 6, he sums up our responsibility this way: "Take up the full armor of God, so that you may be able to resist in the evil day, and having prepared everything, to take your stand" (Eph 6:13 CSB). We win by standing our ground, by staying faithful. When I am in the heat of a spiritual battle, I find myself praying this short prayer over and over: "Lord, I trust you. Give me strength to endure." Sometimes that's all I can pray, but even that small prayer is an act of faith. Prayer really is the primary language of perseverance.

To stress endurance, Revelation also uses the important Greek word *hypomonē*, translated "patient endurance" or with the thought of persevering, seven times in the book: 1:9; 2:2, 3, 19; 3:10; 13:10; 14:12. One Revelation scholar refers to "patient endurance" as "the key ethical term in the Apocalypse."[3]

Let's look at each occurrence briefly. In 1:9, John assures his readers that all Christians share in three important realities: membership in God's kingdom, suffering or tribulation, and *patient endurance*. All of us will experience both the privileges (membership in the kingdom) and responsibilities (suffering and endurance) of living as a Christ follower in this fallen world. In 2:2–3, Jesus commends the church in Ephesus for their hard work and *perseverance*, including their refusal to compromise with false teaching. In 2:19, Jesus praises the Thyatirian Christians for their love, faith, service, and *perseverance*. In 3:10, Jesus promises spiritual protection for those who have kept his command to *persevere*, or *endure patiently*, through trials.

The final two occurrences are especially significant. In 13:1–10, we are introduced to the beast from the sea and told that this person/power will blaspheme God and wage war against (and yes, even temporarily "conquer") God's people (13:6–7). Those who follow the Lamb can expect captivity and the sword (13:9–10). When the culture becomes strongly anti-Christian, persecution is inevitable for faithful believers. As a result, we are told, "This calls for *patient endurance* and faithfulness on the part of God's people" (13:10). God has never promised to remove his people from the fire of trials and persecution, but he has promised to walk with us through the fire as we continue to trust him. He will never leave us or forsake us. He is with us always (Matt 28:20).

In 14:6–11, there are three angelic messages of judgment, followed by a call for endurance and a blessing for believers in 14:12–13:

Call for endurance: "This calls for *patient endurance* on the part of the people of God who keep his commands and remain faithful to Jesus."

Blessing: "'Blessed are the dead who die in the Lord from now on.' 'Yes,' says the Spirit, 'they will rest from their labor, for their deeds will follow them.'"

This seems like a very odd and, can we say, discouraging blessing. The idea of dying in the Lord being a blessing is foreign to our way of thinking. But this reminds us that people actually do overcome and endure and win the victory. They have come through the great trials and persecutions of this world and have remained faithful to the end (7:13–14; 15:2; 21:7). The blessing is telling us that even if our faithfulness costs us our lives, God still has us. He is sovereign even over the last enemy, death (1 Cor 15:26).

How can we possibly get to the place where we are willing to stay faithful unto death? A story from a well-known twentieth-century believer brings me great hope and perspective. Corrie ten Boom, a Dutch Christian, was sent to a German concentration camp for being part of the underground resistance movement that helped Jews escape the evils of Nazi Germany. Corrie endured horrible conditions in the deplorable prisons as she struggled to trust God: bitter cold, lack of food, disease, filth, overcrowding, hard labor. A low point was the death of her sister, Betsie. Corrie confessed years later that her soul was a battleground in the struggle between light and darkness. Especially difficult were the humiliating Friday medical exams when the women had to strip naked. On one particular Friday she remembered something from the Gospels—Jesus hung naked on the cross. He too faced the ridicule and abuse and humiliation of persecutors. She came to see two realities that made suffering bearable. First, God is sovereign. He is in control, and we must trust him. But second, God also suffered in the person of Jesus Christ. He knows what suffering feels

186

like. We can stay steadfast in the face of evil when we recall that our God is both a *sovereign* and a *suffering* God. We need both to keep going.[4]

Saying No to Evil

Revelation not only tells us that we are in a war and that we must endure; it also instructs us with specifics about what to do. In this section, we will see that endurance means saying no to evil. In the next, we learn that it also involves saying yes to Jesus. In other words, if we are to persevere faithfully, we will need to reject some things and embrace others. We really have important ethical choices to make. Living for God has always included both what to do and what not to do, and the same holds true in Revelation.

What specifically does Revelation call us to reject? To begin with, we are to reject false teaching. The seven messages mention false teachers several times: the Nicolaitans, those who hold to the teaching of Balaam, and the prophetess Jezebel (2:20–23). All three probably refer to false teachers who were redefining the Christian faith to allow believers to fit in with (and perhaps even profit from) the prevailing pagan culture. They likely encouraged Christians to join the local trade guilds and participate in the pagan worship rituals connected to emperor worship, assuring them that such activities would not harm their faith. But Jesus hates this false teaching and commends the church at Ephesus for doing the same (2:6). He chastises the church at Pergamum for tolerating the false teachers and warns them to repent (2:14–15). And in Thyatira, Jesus encourages the faithful Christians who have rejected Jezebel's teachings (2:24–28), pronounces judgment on her and her devoted followers (2:23), and warns the Christians who are toying with her ideas (2:22).

Revelation warns us not to dabble in false teaching. We're playing with fire when we do so. Often, false teaching comes from those who claim a secretive, deeper kind of religious experience or from those who suggest that it's okay to redefine the historic Christian faith in order to be accepted by the surrounding society. In both cases, the truth of God's Word often takes a backseat to personal experience or worldly trends. We find ourselves trying to make God and his Word fit into our lives rather than adjusting our lives to match God's ways. If you're in that place right now, please remember that there are no earthly advantages or pleasures that can be compared to what God has in store for those who love him.

Closely related to rejecting false teaching is the call to reject the worship of false gods, a practice we often call idolatry. The famous "mark of the beast" of Revelation 13 is a symbol of ownership, identification, and allegiance (13:16–17). Just as believers display the seal of the living God now, not literally but through the overall direction of our lives (7:1–8), so unbelievers will bear the mark of the beast, a figurative sign of their idolatry evidenced through their actions (right hand) and their thinking (forehead). In our society, money and power are often connected to false worship. Notice in Revelation 13 that those who refuse to worship the beast can no longer buy or sell, meaning that they will suffer economically. Don't be surprised if this is how the temptation presents itself to us as well. Are we willing to give up material comforts or financial security in order to follow Jesus Christ? As Jesus himself says, "No one can serve two masters. Either you will hate the one and love the other, or you will be devoted to the one and despise the other. You cannot serve both God and money" (Matt 6:24).

Revelation also calls us to reject the wicked behavior of people who don't know God. The book includes three formal lists that detail the type of ungodly behavior that God condemns.

> The rest of mankind who were not killed by these plagues still did not repent of the work of their hands; they did not stop

worshiping demons, and idols of gold, silver, bronze, stone and wood—idols that cannot see or hear or walk. Nor did they repent of their murders, their magic arts, their sexual immorality or their thefts. (9:20–21)

But the cowardly, the unbelieving, the vile, the murderers, the sexually immoral, those who practice magic arts, the idolaters and all liars—they will be consigned to the fiery lake of burning sulfur. This is the second death. (21:8)

Outside are the dogs, those who practice magic arts, the sexually immoral, the murderers, the idolaters and everyone who loves and practices falsehood. (22:15)

Such are the ongoing practices of people who will be excluded from God's presence forever because they don't have a relationship with him. In these lists of sins, we see a complete breakdown of a person's relationship to God as well as their relationships to other people. This is the exact opposite of the greatest commandment, to love God and love people (Mark 12:29–31). In Rev 18:4, God's people are called to run for their lives away from the sins of Babylon, the center of pagan power: "Then I heard another voice from heaven say: 'Come out of her, my people,' so that you will not share in her sins, so that you will not receive any of her plagues." One aspect of holiness is a separation from the world system as part of our separation unto the Lord.

Let's say you've been reading about all that we should reject—false teaching, idolatry, sexual immorality, materialism, lying, and deceit—and you're ashamed to say that you see patterns of such behavior in your own life. Well, the good news is that Jesus tells his people in the seven churches to change their thinking and behavior, and this gives us hope for change as well. The operative word here, though not popular or politically correct, is "repentance." To repent means to change. Jesus exhorts the Christians at Ephesus, Pergamum,

Thyatira, Sardis, and Laodicea to repent (2:5, 16, 22; 3:3, 19). Repentance involves a change of mind and heart, a rejection of the ungodly behavior, and a genuine redirection of future thinking and actions. When Jesus commands his people to repent in Revelation, he usually adds a stern warning of future judgment if there is no repentance (2:5, 16, 22–23; 3:3).

Jesus's words to the church in Laodicea are especially relevant. To a group of Christians in need of a lot of change, he says in 3:19–20, "Those whom I love I rebuke and discipline. So be earnest and repent. Here I am! I stand at the door and knock. If anyone hears my voice and opens the door, I will come in and eat with that person, and they with me."

Many believers today have tried to live in their own strength and failed miserably. Now, as they become aware of their need for restoration, the lingering question is, Does God still want a relationship with me now in light of all that I've done? Jesus's love means that he hasn't abandoned you or written you off. Instead, he waits to offer forgiveness and restoration if you will turn away from your prideful self-reliance and open your heart to him. In the ancient world, sharing a meal together in someone's home indicated a strong friendship. Jesus's promise of a fellowship meal means he offers real forgiveness. By continuously knocking on the door of your heart, he is saying, "Yes, I want to renew our relationship. I've been here all along. If you hear me knocking and open your life to me, I'll come in and bring healing and restoration." He wants to make things right, but the door only opens from the inside.

Saying Yes to Jesus

On the night before he died on the cross, Jesus said to his disciples, "If you love me, keep my commands" (John 14:15), and "Whoever has my commands and keeps them is the one who loves me" (John 14:21). Revelation also sends the message

190

that to love God means to obey him. Just to be clear, we can't obey our way into a relationship with God. Rather, we obey as a result of all that God has done for us in Christ (i.e., "We love because he first loved us," 1 John 4:19).

Revelation even describes Christians as those who "keep God's commands" (12:17; cf. 14:12). Obedience is the chief characteristic of a Christian. That is who we are: obedient children. We keep Jesus's command to endure patiently (3:8, 10). We obey the prophecy (1:3; 22:7, 9). We love and serve and trust God and persevere (2:13, 19). And we bear witness to Jesus (6:9; 11:3; 12:11, 17; 17:6; 19:10; 20:4).

Through vivid picture language, Revelation also stresses the importance of obedience. As a member of the bride of Christ, every believer is clothed in righteousness in preparation for the great marriage celebration of the Lamb that occurs at Jesus's second coming. This refers not only to God's gift of righteousness but also to our own righteous acts done in response to God's grace (19:7–8): "'Let us rejoice and be glad and give him glory! For the wedding of the Lamb has come, and his bride has made herself ready. Fine linen, bright and clean, was given her [the bride of Christ] to wear.'" (Fine linen stands for the righteous acts of God's holy people.)

In the ancient world, to be unclothed meant to be unprepared to face God's judgment. To be naked symbolized shame and guilt. Jesus says in 16:15, "Look, I come like a thief! Blessed is the one who stays awake and remains clothed, so as not to go naked and be shamefully exposed." Jesus commends the faithful few in Sardis who "have not soiled their clothes. They will walk with me, dressed in white, for they are worthy" (3:4). There is also a blessing in 22:14 on "those who wash their robes, that they may have the right to the tree of life and may go through the gates into the city." Christians are people robed in righteousness, and this image includes both God's gracious gift and our response of loving obedience to Christ.

Revelation establishes a strong connection between eschatology (thinking about the end times) and ethics (how we live now). Those who anticipate and long for Christ's return are called to holy living. Our obedience matters since it reflects the genuineness of our faith. The book even closes with a summary statement about the two kinds of people there are in this world: righteous and wicked (22:10–11): "Then he told me, 'Do not seal up the words of the prophecy of this scroll, because the time is near. Let the one who does wrong continue to do wrong; let the vile person continue to be vile; let the one who does right continue to do right; and let the holy person continue to be holy.'" But if you're like me, trying hard to obey a bunch of rules actually paralyzes me and causes me to be less obedient in the long run, if that makes any sense. I can sometimes lose perspective when I focus on obedience. Instead, it helps me tremendously to focus on Jesus rather than on doing things for him. Everything becomes much more personal and full of life when I focus on staying loyal and faithful to the person of Christ. Fixing our eyes on Jesus and on him alone has even helped those who have suffered the most to persevere (Heb 12:2).

Dietrich Bonhoeffer once preached a chapel sermon based on Revelation 14, titled "Learning to Die." Bonhoeffer talked about how Babylon the Great (the evil empire that opposed God) would be defeated and eventually crumble because it had already been defeated by Christ on the cross. As a result, Bonhoeffer told his listeners, you have nothing to fear. Bonhoeffer said, "Do not fear the coming day, do not fear other people, do not fear power or might, even if they are able to deprive you of property and life; do not fear the great ones of this world; do not even fear yourselves." God is greater than all our fears. Bonhoeffer urged his listeners to cling to Jesus to the very end. He closed by saying,

> To die in Christ—that this be granted us, that our last hour not be a weak hour, that we die as confessors of Christ, whether

old or young, whether quickly or after long suffering, whether seized and laid hold of by the lord of Babylon. . . . That is our prayer today, that our last word might only be: Christ.[5]

It Will Be Worth It

It's not unspiritual to ask bold questions. Why should I persevere? What is the reward for enduring to the end? Why not just lie and get the extra money so that the bill collectors will stop hounding us? Why not give in to the pleasures that everyone else seems to be enjoying rather than exercise self-control? Why continue to pray when the situation seems hopeless? Why not accept our culture's ever-changing definition of truth rather than hold on to the ancient truth of the Bible and offend people? Why believe that Jesus is the only true God when all these other religions claim a path to God? Why love people who ridicule me? Why serve people who exclude me? Perseverance is hard. Hanging on is killing me. Why should I keep slogging through all this mess? Why should I stay faithful?

Why endure? Two reasons. First, we persevere because God commands us to do so. Second, we endure because Jesus promises that it will be worth it in the end.

Revelation reminds us that Jesus will (eventually) reward us for staying faithful. That's right—the rewards are almost all rewards that come on that final day rather than right now. Because we typically think of a reward as something to be received now rather than later, these eternal rewards sometimes don't grip us as they should. It's hard to be motivated by heavenly rewards that don't seem to change our circumstances now. We can be tremendously shortsighted, having been conditioned by our culture to delay nothing. We want our rewards here and now. But God doesn't play by our rules. God seems unbothered by hurry. He detests quick fixes and shortcuts. He works in deep ways over long periods of time to refine and shape our character and accomplish his plans. He knows what is best and sees our life and the whole world from an eternal perspective, whereas we see only what is right in front of us. But the more you think about these final rewards, the more they begin to bear the weight they were meant to bear, and the more meaningful they become to us now.

At the end of each of the seven messages to the churches, Jesus promises rewards to those who persevere. Although the details of these rewards are sometimes unclear, let me summarize the main ideas:

	Image	Meaning
2:7	Eat from the tree of life in the paradise of God	Guarantee of eternal life
2:11	Not be hurt at all by the second death	Resurrection life rather than eternal death
2:17	Receive hidden manna and a white stone with a new name on it	God's eternal acceptance, care, and provision
2:26–28	Authority over the nations and the morning star	Sharing with Jesus in ruling over the heavenly kingdom
3:5	Dressed in white and our name in the book of life and acknowledged by Jesus before the Father	Secure and permanent citizenship in God's eternal kingdom and Jesus's personal acknowledgment and commendation
3:12	A pillar in God's temple and three new names	A special relationship with the triune God and life forever in his presence
3:21	Right to sit with Jesus on his throne	A share in Christ's victory and authority

These are amazingly important rewards. We couldn't make a list of rewards that surpasses this list. How could God give us anything more?

We learn about those rewards in the first few chapters of Revelation, but the rest of the book also highlights eternal rewards for those who persevere to the end. There are seven beatitudes found in Revelation—the "blessed are" statements. Two of the blessings are given to those who read and obey the book (1:3; 22:7), but the other five are eternal blessings reserved for those who persevere: the presence of God (14:13), being prepared for Jesus's return (16:15), an invitation to the wedding supper of the Lamb (19:9), sharing in the resurrection and avoiding the second death (20:6), eating of the tree of life and entering the eternal city (22:14).

The very end of the book also stresses the rewards God has in store for those who love him. Those who endure will inherit the new creation that is described in chapters 21–22 (21:7, 27). We will enjoy the life, health, and abundance of the new heaven and new earth, and most of all, the presence of God (22:3–5, 14). These rewards will be ours when Jesus returns (22:12).

For now, we persevere and we wait. It's unbelievably difficult for some. What God has in store for you will make all the suffering worth it. The apostle Paul's words in Romans capture the message of Revelation well: "The sufferings of this present time are not worth comparing with the glory that is going to be revealed to us. . . . Now if we hope for what we do not see, we eagerly wait for it with patience" (Rom 8:18, 25 CSB). To look forward to what God has promised is not irresponsible or foolish; it's what the Bible calls hope. We wait in hope because we trust our God.

Conclusion

Perseverance is rarely easy. It's normally tough to hang in there over the long haul. The Christian life is not a short sprint but a long-distance race. My favorite hobby is cycling, and I've ridden a bunch of centuries, or one-hundred-mile rides. The first ten to fifteen miles are effortless. I don't really begin getting tired until about thirty miles or so. I usually start to hurt after about sixty miles, and the struggle lasts until the end. In the last part of any long ride, I experience two strong emotions: I want to do my very best, and I want to quit—both at the same time. I have to force myself to drink and eat when that's the last thing I want to do. I have to tell myself over and over to "keep on pedaling" and that the finish line is just ahead.

There are many parallels between cycling and the Christian life, but two stand out. First, the race is hard. The Christian life is not easy, and we should expect life in a broken world to be tough at times. Yes, following Jesus is always worth it because it's the only way we can experience true life, but that doesn't make it easy or effortless. I enter every race knowing that it will be a test but also knowing it will be worth it in the end. The same is true for our journey as Christians.

The second parallel is that we're not in this alone. I always ride centuries with a group. When you ride just behind another cyclist, you save about 30 percent of your energy. We take turns being the lead rider so that others can draft behind us, but we also allow others to pull us along so that we can recover. Trying to live the Christian life apart from a healthy Christian community is not only hard; it borders on the impossible.

At the beginning of Revelation John describes his circumstances in this way: "I, John, your brother and companion in the suffering and kingdom and patient endurance that are ours in Jesus, was on the island of Patmos because of the word of God and the testimony of Jesus" (1:9). Don't miss that all these things are "ours" in Jesus—not just John's, but "ours." John is our "brother and companion" in suffering, in the kingdom, and in patient endurance—the bad, the good, and the difficult. We share all this together. We endure as community. We can't make it alone. We need each other, and God has given us a community to help us persevere. Sometimes we'll be out front hitting the headwind so that others can recover. At other times, we'll rely on the strength of others. We'll need their example, their prayers, their forgiveness, and their encouragement to make it. We're in this together, and we persevere as a community. We don't have to go it alone.

196

In this chapter, Revelation has reminded us that we're in a real spiritual battle, facing both opposition and temptation. We win the victory by enduring. To persevere is to win! Overcoming involves saying no to evil and yes to Jesus. We don't have to achieve the victory ourselves; we just have to rely on the victory that Christ has already won. And God promises that it will all be worth it in the end. The precious, newborn baby doesn't make the mother forget all the pains of childbirth, but the little one sure makes the pains purposeful. What God has in store for us in the new creation will make all the pains of perseverance worth it.

Key texts: Rev 2:10; 12:11, 17; 14:12–13; 22:12–21
Reading plan: Revelation 2–3; 11–12

Community Group Questions

1. What do you think most of your friends expect of the Christian life? Have you ever had to change your expectations about the Christian life? If so, what caused the change?

2. For Christians in your church, do you think opposition or temptation is the greater threat? Why?

3. How do the pressures of life in the ancient Roman Empire seem to parallel the pressures we face today?

4. In Revelation, we overcome or win the victory by enduring. How can we redefine "winning" to give us a more biblical mind-set?

5. Why is it important to embrace both saying no to evil and saying yes to Jesus as part of perseverance?

6. How can we see our future hope more clearly so that it helps us endure our present circumstances?

7. What is the most important truth you have learned in this chapter about perseverance?

NOTES

Introduction

1. I've taken some of the information in this section from my commentary on Revelation. See J. Scott Duvall, *Revelation*, Teach the Text Commentary Series (Grand Rapids: Baker Books, 2014).

2. For more on how to interpret the Bible in context, see J. Scott Duvall and J. Daniel Hays, *Grasping God's Word: A Hands-On Approach to Reading, Interpreting, and Applying the Bible*, 3rd ed. (Grand Rapids: Zondervan, 2012), and its abridgment, Duvall and Hays, *Journey into God's Word: Your Guide to Understanding and Applying the Bible* (Grand Rapids: Zondervan, 2008).

3. If you want to read more about how to interpret Revelation as prophetic-apocalyptic literature, see Duvall and Hays, *Grasping God's Word*, 309–30.

Cast of Characters in the Divine Drama of Revelation

1. This cast of characters is from Duvall, *Revelation*, 311–13 (see intro., n. 1).

Chapter 1: God

1. C. S. Lewis, *George MacDonald: An Anthology* (New York: Harper-Collins, 2001), 103.

2. Mark Wilson, *Victory through the Lamb: A Guide to Revelation in Plain Language* (Wooster, OH: Weaver Books, 2014), 9.

3. Just as the first readers were a minority in their culture, so evangelical Christians are now a minority in American culture, whether we admit it or not. See John S. Dickerson, *The Great Evangelical Recession: 6 Factors That Will Crash the American Church . . . and How to Prepare* (Grand Rapids: Baker Books, 2013). We can fret about our lack of influence, but ultimately our security lies in God's almighty kingship over all. He's in control now and one day will set everything right.

4. Eric Metaxas, *Bonhoeffer: Pastor, Martyr, Prophet, Spy* (Nashville: Thomas Nelson, 2010); Paul Marshall, Lela Gilbert, and Nina Shea, *Persecuted: The Global Assault on Christians* (Nashville: Thomas Nelson, 2013); https://www.opendoorsusa.org/; http://www.persecution.com/.

5. A term used nine times in Revelation: 1:8; 4:8; 11:17; 15:3; 16:7, 14; 19:6, 15; 21:22.

6. Richard J. Bauckham, *The Theology of Revelation* (Cambridge: Cambridge University Press, 1993), 40.

7. Bauckham, 46.

8. In 1757 at age twenty-two, Robert Robinson wrote the hymn "Come Thou Fount of Every Blessing," which features this stanza: "O to grace how great a debtor, daily I'm constrained to be! Let Thy goodness, like a fetter, bind my wandering heart to Thee. Prone to wander, Lord, I feel it, prone to leave the God I love; Here's my heart, O take and *seal* it, *seal* it for Thy courts above."

9. Alan Kent Scholes, *What Christianity Is All About: How You Can Know and Enjoy God* (Colorado Springs: NavPress, 1999), 55–57.

10. The promise of God's presence is repeated many times in Scripture (e.g., Gen 17:7; Exod 6:7; 2 Cor 6:16). At times all three parts are mentioned, and at other times just one or two. For more on this important promise, see Walter C. Kaiser Jr., *The Promise Plan of God: A Biblical Theology of the Old and New Testaments* (Grand Rapids: Zondervan, 2008). See also J. Scott Duvall and J. Daniel Hays, *The Relational Presence of God: The Cohesive Center of Biblical Theology* (Grand Rapids: Baker Academic, forthcoming).

11. For more discussion of "tabernacle" and the idea of God's presence dwelling among us, see "The Holy Spirit in the Heavenly City" in chap. 4.

12. Westminster Shorter Catechism, question 1 (emphasis added).

13. For more on this idea, see chap. 2, "Seeing the Big Picture," in Henry Cloud and John Townsend, *How People Grow: What the Bible Reveals about Personal Growth* (Grand Rapids: Zondervan, 2009).

Chapter 2: Worship

1. G. K. Beale and Mitchell Kim, *God Dwells among Us: Expanding Eden to the Ends of the Earth* (Downers Grove, IL: InterVarsity, 2014), 118.

2. I heard Musburger make the comment myself while I was watching the game; SEC Network, August 28, 2014.

3. Augustine, *Confessions*, bk 1.

4. Eugene Peterson, *Reversed Thunder: The Revelation of John and the Praying Imagination* (New York: HarperSanFrancisco, 1988), 59.

5. The Greek term *latreuō* ("serve") is actually translated "worship" in other places in the New Testament: Luke 2:37; Acts 7:7, 42; 24:14; Heb 9:9; 10:2; 12:28.

6. Bob Kauflin, *Worship Matters: Leading Others to Encounter the Greatness of God* (Wheaton, IL: Crossway, 2008), 26.

7. Bauckham, *The Theology of Revelation*, 51 (see chap. 1, n. 6).

8. See Duvall, *Revelation*, 120 (see intro., n. 1).

Chapter 3: The People of God

1. Mark Wilson, "Revelation," in *Zondervan Illustrated Bible Backgrounds Commentary*, ed. Cinton E. Arnold (Grand Rapids: Zondervan, 2002), 4:265.
2. For more discussion of "endurance" in Revelation, see chap. 10.
3. Marshall, Gilbert, and Shea, *Persecuted*, 4 (see chap. 1, n. 4); see 6–7 for the list and consequences that follow.
4. For the details on Revelation 11, see Duvall, *Revelation*, 148–53 (see intro., n. 1). For even more information, see the fine work by my friend Rob Dalrymple, *Revelation and the Two Witnesses* (Eugene, OR: Wipf & Stock, 2011).
5. The term "persecution" or "tribulation" (*thlipsis*) is used in 2:9–10, where it refers to Christians suffering physically. In 1:9, John says that he is a companion with other believers in "suffering." In 7:14, John sees the great multitude, the church, which has come out of the "great tribulation" and is now in heaven, praising God. It is used in 2:22 of the suffering of Jezebel.

Chapter 4: The Holy Spirit

1. Frederick Dale Bruner and William Hordern, *Holy Spirit: Shy Member of the Trinity* (Eugene, OR: Wipf & Stock, 2001).
2. For more on the significance of numbers in Revelation, see Duvall, *Revelation*, 163 (see intro., n. 1).
3. Metaxas, *Bonhoeffer*, 528, 532 (see chap. 1, n. 4).

Chapter 5: Our Enemies

1. *The Martyrdom of Polycarp*, trans. J. B. Lightfoot, ed. Stephen Tomkins; see "#103: Polycarp's Martyrdom," ed. Dan Graves, Christian History Institute, https://www.christianhistoryinstitute.org/study/module/polycarp/).
2. Cindy Wooden, "Persecution of Christians Worse Than in Early Church, Says Francis," *Catholic Herald*, June 23, 2014, http://www.catholicherald.co.uk/news/2014/06/23/persecution-of-christians-worse-than-in-early-church-says-francis/.
3. Go to http://www.persecution.com or http://www.persecution.org to learn more about how Christians are being persecuted today and how you can support them.
4. See Duvall, *Revelation*, 223–24 (see intro., n. 1).
5. The following illustration is taken from J. Scott Duvall, *Experiencing God's Story of Life and Hope: A Workbook for Spiritual Formation* (Grand Rapids: Kregel, 2008), 19.
6. See Duvall, *Revelation*, 186–87.
7. See Duvall, *Revelation*, 180, on how the healing of this death wound imitates Christ's resurrection:
   Many interpreters believe the fatal wound that was healed refers to a Roman emperor, most likely Nero. After Nero committed suicide in

AD 68, rumors spread that he had not actually died. Rather, he had escaped to the east and would one day come back with an army to return to power. Others believed that Nero had died and would rise from the dead (the *Nero redivivus* myth). The most viable attempts to understand how this text communicates beyond the first century include (1) the repeated rise of pagan political, military, and economic powers that oppose God and his people, and (2) the death and apparent resurrection of the antichrist himself at the end of the age.

8. Cornelius Plantinga, *Not the Way It's Supposed to Be: A Breviary of Sin* (Grand Rapids: Eerdmans, 1995), 98.

9. See my comments on Revelation 20 in Duvall, *Revelation*, 262–79.

10. Grant R. Osborne, *Revelation*, Baker Exegetical Commentary on the New Testament (Grand Rapids: Baker Academic, 2002), 34.

11. See J. Scott Duvall, "Revelation: The Transforming Vision," in C. Marvin Pate et al., *The Story of Israel: A Biblical Theology* (Downers Grove, IL: InterVarsity, 2004), 254–77.

12. C. S. Lewis, *The Lion, the Witch and the Wardrobe*, The Chronicles of Narnia (New York: HarperCollins, 1982), 185.

Chapter 6: The Mission

1. Bruce W. Longenecker, *The Lost Letters of Pergamum: A Story from the New Testament World*, 2nd ed. (Grand Rapids: Baker Academic, 2016).

2. If you're interested in the key words for "witness" in Revelation, they are: "testimony" (*martyria*—1:2, 9; 6:9; 11:7; 12:11, 17; 19:10; 20:4); "witness" (*martys*—1:5; 2:13; 3:14; 11:3; 17:6 [see CSB]); "bear witness, testify" (*martyreō*—1:2; 22:16, 18 [see CSB], 20); "testimony" (*martyrion*—15:5 [see CSB]).

3. Redeemed Gentiles coming into the heavenly city also fulfill Old Testament passages such as Isaiah 60; 61:6; Jer 3:17; Zech 2:11; 8:22–23.

4. R. Kent Hughes, *Acts: The Church Afire*, Preaching the Word (Wheaton: Crossway, 1996), 149.

5. Martin Luther King Jr., interview, *Meet the Press*, April 17, 1960, https://kinginstitute.stanford.edu/king-papers/documents/interview-meet-press.

6. For persuasive reasons for interpreting the two witnesses as the entire community of faith, see G. K. Beale, *The Book of Revelation*, New International Greek Testament Commentary (Grand Rapids: Eerdmans, 1999), 572–75; and Craig S. Keener, *Revelation*, NIV Application Commentary (Grand Rapids: Zondervan, 2000), 291–92. For an outstanding study of Revelation 11, see Dalrymple, *Revelation and the Two Witnesses* (see chap. 3, n. 4).

7. These three themes condense the four themes that Dalrymple sees in Revelation 11. See Dalrymple, *Revelation and the Two Witnesses*, 47–58.

8. Metaxas, *Bonhoeffer*, 192 (see chap. 1, n. 4).

9. Dietrich Bonhoeffer, *The Cost of Discipleship*, rev. ed. (New York: Macmillan, 1963), 99.

10. For a lengthy discussion of the problems associated with interpreting 14:4 literally and why the figurative reading is much preferred, see Beale, *Revelation*, 737–41. In addition, unfaithfulness in the Old Testament is often described as adultery (e.g., Jer 3:1–10; 13:27; Ezek 16:15–58; 23:1–49; Hos 5:4; 6:10).

Chapter 7: Jesus Christ

1. Bauckham, *The Theology of Revelation*, 63 (see chap. 1, n. 6).
2. John Stott, *The Cross of Christ* (Downers Grove, IL: InterVarsity, 2006), 151–52.
3. See Stott, chap. 6.
4. Robert H. Mounce, *The Book of Revelation*, rev. ed., New International Commentary on the New Testament (Grand Rapids: Eerdmans, 1998), 356.

Chapter 8: Judgment

1. Bryan M. Litfin, *Early Christian Martyr Stories: An Evangelical Introduction with New Translations* (Grand Rapids: Baker Academic, 2014), 84–85.
2. Mounce, *The Book of Revelation*, 320 (see chap. 7, n. 4).
3. C. S. Lewis, *The Screwtape Letters* (New York: HarperCollins, 2001), 38–39.
4. Osborne, *Revelation*, 39–40 (see chap. 5, n. 10).
5. For more on the two witnesses and the church, see "The Church as a Community of Faithful Witnesses" in chap. 6 and its notes.
6. Some scholars see this first vision as a positive vision of harvesting believers from the earth. For more on this, see J. Scott Duvall, *Revelation*, Teach the Text Commentary Series (Grand Rapids: Baker Books, 2014), 203.
7. Francis Chan and Preston Sprinkle, *Erasing Hell: What God Said about Eternity, and the Things We've Made Up* (Colorado Springs: David C. Cook, 2011), 107–8.
8. C. S. Lewis, *The Great Divorce* (New York: Macmillan, 1946), 75.

Chapter 9: The New Creation

1. If you want to know more about how the whole Bible fits together into one big story, see J. Scott Duvall and J. Daniel Hays, *Living God's Word: Discovering Our Place in the Great Story of Scripture* (Grand Rapids: Zondervan, 2012).
2. I am indebted to Wayne Martindale for this concept. See his wonderful book *Beyond the Shadowlands: C. S. Lewis on Heaven and Hell* (Wheaton, IL: Crossway, 2005), esp. chap. 1, "The Myths of Heaven Exposed."
3. Cornelius Plantinga, *Not the Way It's Supposed to Be: A Breviary of Sin* (Grand Rapids: Eerdmans, 1995), 10 (italics original).

4. C. S. Lewis, *Mere Christianity* (New York: Simon & Schuster, 1996), 119. Since there are so many editions of Lewis's classic, it might help to know you can find this quote on the first page of chap. 10, dealing with "Hope."

Chapter 10: Perseverance

1. For a well-documented account of the persecution of Christians worldwide, see Marshall, Gilbert, and Shea, *Persecuted* (see chap. 1, n. 4).

2. See Duvall, "Revelation," in Pate et al., *The Story of Israel*, 276 (see chap. 5, n. 11).

3. Osborne, *Revelation*, 543 (see chap. 5, n. 10).

4. For this insight, see Jim Belcher, *In Search of Deep Faith: A Pilgrimage into the Beauty, Goodness and Heart of Christianity* (Downers Grove, IL: InterVarsity, 2013), 221.

5. From "Learning to Die," in *A Testament of Freedom: The Essential Writings of Dietrich Bonhoeffer*, ed. Geffrey B. Kelly and F. Burton Nelson (San Francisco: HarperSanFrancisco, 1995), 265–68. Quoted in Belcher, *In Search of Deep Faith*, 238–39.

SUBJECT INDEX

beatitudes (or "blessings") of
Revelation, seven, 98–99,
194–195
behavior that God condemns,
188–189
Bible
one of the clearest definitions of
discipleship, 116
one of the most comforting sections, 64–65
black horse, 152
Blandina (second-century martyr), 140
blessings
of religious liberty, 179–180
of Revelation, seven, 98–99,
194–195
blood
of the Lamb, 57, 92, 99, 117,
131, 168, 176, 184
water turning to, 146, 152
bloodshed, 17, 144, 152
Bonhoeffer, Dietrich, 77–78, 113,
192–193
Bonhoeffer (Metaxas), 24, 77
book of life, 14, 88, 100, 127,
154, 163, 194
bowls / bowl judgments, 33, 143,
146, 151, 152, 156–157
Bridegroom, 45, 121, 168
bride of Christ, 14, 15, 19, 45,
54, 64, 72, 73, 116, 121,
127, 162, 164, 168–169,
175, 176, 191
Burke, Edmund, 141

C
Caesar, 4, 7–8, 18, 88, 182
Chan, Francis, 155
cherubim, 15
Chesterton, G. K., 21

Christian, chief characteristic of,
191
Christology, 122
churches
singing in evangelical, 49
what the Spirit was saying to
the, 74–75
church, the (body of Christ), 2, 4,
10, 14, 15, 16, 45, 58, 59,
66, 73, 81, 89, 113, 119,
121, 127, 162, 168, 169,
180, 183, 201
as a community of faithful witnesses, 109–114
expectation in the contemporary American, 179
one of the biggest lies being
thrown at the American,
63
why the world hates the, 58–59
city
great, 15
holy, 15, 17, 64, 143, 164, 169,
175
Holy Spirit in the heavenly,
79–83
clouds, 134
coins, 5, 7, 25, 56
commands, 56, 59, 75, 114–115,
118, 186, 190–191
community
God's covenant community,
53–67
God's promises of, 31
life was meant to be lived in, 65
compromise, 75, 99
conquering, the recipe for overcoming and, 57
consumerism, 105, 183
context, 2, 3, 10, 60, 68, 103,
112, 153, 182, 199

N
nakedness, 96
Narnia, 171
nations, 16–17, 25, 31, 38, 42,
     46, 55, 62, 63, 95, 116,
     135, 136, 144, 146, 149,
     153, 161, 162, 163, 167,
     176, 194
  God's love for, 104–107, 119
Nazi Germany, 14, 186
Nazis, 77, 112, 182
Nero (emperor), 3, 14, 18, 24, 87,
     93, 201
new creation, 2, 14, 15, 17, 19,
     26, 28, 31, 32, 76, 80, 85,
     105, 136, 156, 159–177,
     180, 195, 197
new heaven and new earth, 7, 15,
     17, 32, 79, 83, 97, 131,
     132, 154, 159–177, 195
new Jerusalem, 1, 9, 15, 17,
     64–65, 67, 73, 80, 105,
     164, 167, 169
new song, 17, 46, 126, 128–129,
     170
Nicolaitans, 6, 17, 86–87, 187
Niemöller, Martin, 112
Nike (goddess), 56
number of the beast's name, 18

O
obedience, 55, 96, 108, 114–116,
     191–192
offspring (of the sun-clothed
     woman), 19, 58, 59, 91,
     114
olive trees, 19, 109
144,000, the, 1, 15, 17, 54, 123,
     126, 170
Open Doors, 24
Osborne, Grant, 97, 146
overcomers, requirements for, 99

overcoming, the recipe for, 57

P
paganism, 87
pale horse, 152
Passover lamb (of Exodus), 16
Patmos, 4, 8, 53, 104, 117, 196
Paul (apostle), 28, 32, 59, 65, 76,
     80–81, 89, 90, 106, 145,
     173, 182, 184, 195
people of god, 53–67
Pergamum, 103–104, 182, 187,
     189–190
Persecuted (Marshall, Gilbert,
     and Shea), 24, 58
persecution, 5, 6, 18, 24, 28, 30,
     46, 56, 57, 59, 60, 61, 63,
     66, 75, 77, 85, 87, 89, 91,
     94, 99–100, 101, 109,
     111, 112, 113, 139, 148,
     156, 179, 180–182, 185,
     186, 201, 204
perseverance, 2, 57, 60, 117–119,
     126, 179–197
Peter, Saint, 151, 159
Peterson, Eugene, 38
Philadelphia (of Asia Minor), 6,
     112, 118
Plantinga, Cornelius, 94–95
Polycarp, 24, 87–88
posture (in worship), 48
prayer
  effects of, 147–148
  language of perseverance, 119,
     184
prayers, 28, 29, 147–148, 196
presence, God's, 9, 15, 19, 22,
     32, 39, 42, 64–65, 67,
     71, 76, 78, 79–82, 91, 98,
     121, 124, 127, 134, 142,
     143, 147, 154, 160, 162,
     163, 164, 165, 166, 169,

172–176, 189, 194, 195, 200

pressure
  three sources of (for early Christians), 4–5
  to conform
    modern-day, 58, 183
    why the churches of Revelation felt, 182–183
  two responses to, 6
promise(s)
  God's three-part (OT), 30, 161
  to victors in Revelation, 160
prophecy, 8, 73, 74, 98, 99, 115, 191, 192
prostitute (of Babylon), 15, 16, 47, 73, 88, 89, 105, 111, 114, 116, 145, 149
  four sins, 89
protection, 18, 23, 64, 78, 87, 109, 112–113, 119, 126, 174, 185

R

Ram, 133–134, 137, 150
Red horse, 152
repentance, 104, 153, 157, 189–190
"repent," meaning of the word, 189
requirements for overcomers, 99
resurrection, 113–114
  first (resurrection of the church), 98, 113, 143, 154, 160, 164
  of Jesus Christ, 17, 18, 32, 59, 61, 85–86, 91, 100, 108, 128, 131–132, 137, 184, 201
return of Christ, 7, 18, 60, 94, 96, 113, 121, 133–136, 137,

151, 153, 183, 184, 192, 195

Revelation
  and Genesis, contrasted, 162–163
  audience of, 8–9
  author of, 121
  Christology of, 122
  helpful guidelines for interpreting the book of, 9–10
  main theme, 121
  seven beatitudes (or "blessings"), 98–99, 194
  summary of the whole message of, 7
  ten most important themes in, 2–3
  three types of literature used to communicate the message of, 8–9
  two popular responses (and a third promising response) to, 1–2
reward(s), 127, 133, 135, 136, 154, 180, 193–195
riders of the Apocalypse, 1, 144
river(s) (of life / living water), 81, 105, 106, 124, 127, 173
robes, 99, 133, 135, 153, 168, 191
Roman Empire, 4, 7, 24, 25, 50, 89, 93, 182
Rome, 4, 7, 9, 13, 14, 15, 24, 25, 33, 89

S

Sardis, 71, 168, 182, 190, 191
Satan (aka the devil), 6, 10, 13, 14, 16, 17, 24, 30, 32, 33, 38, 58–59, 60, 65, 66–67, 78, 85, 86, 87, 90–93, 94,

W

water of life, 65, 72, 124, 127, 166, 173

wedding supper of the Lamb, 15, 19, 98, 153, 163, 175, 195

weddings, first-century Jewish, 175

Westminster Shorter Catechism, 32

white clothing, 168

white horse, 1, 135, 152, 153

wife of the Lamb, 10, 14

Wilson, Mark (Revelation scholar), 24

winepress of God's wrath, 135, 149, 150, 153

witness

Jesus, the faithful, 107–108

supreme expression of Jesus's, 108

three things Revelation tells us, 110–113

what it means to be a faithful, 110–111

witnesses

faithful, 54, 104

church as a community of, 109–114

ethical life of, 114–117

responsibilities as, 119

two, 1, 19, 61, 99, 109, 110, 111, 112, 113, 148, 181, 202

woman

who sits on seven hills, 9

work, 171–172

works of the flesh, 77

Wormwood, 152

worship, 37–50

defined, 38

five main things Revelation tells us, 50

heart of, 41

heartbeat and business of heaven, 39

holistic response, 48

response to God's character, 41

response to God's mighty acts, 42–45

response to God's victory over evil, 46–48

wrath (God's), defined, 140

Z

Zechariah (prophet), 71

SCRIPTURE INDEX

Matthew

3:16 *82*
5:11 *89*
5:44–45 *157*
6 *26*
6:10 *114*
6:24 *188*
12:28 *82*
13:1–23 *74*
18:16 *109*
24:43 *96*
25:41 *91*
28:18–20 *62*
28:19 *106, 120*
28:20 *185*

Mark

2:19–20 *168*
8:34 *108*
8:34–35 *100*
12:29–31 *189*
14:36 *135*

Luke

6:26 *60*
12:39 *96*
19:10 *62*

John

1:14 *32, 79, 172, 174*
1:29 *128*
3:16 *104*
3:29 *168*
4:4–26 *81*
7:37–39 *81*
10:10 *145*
10:11 *127*
10:30 *125*
12:31 *59*
13:23 *27*
14:15 *190*
14:21 *75, 190*

14:26 *69, 72*
15:26 *69, 72*
16:7–15 *72*
16:13–14 *69*
16:33 *66, 113, 180*
17 *81*
17:15 *113*

Acts

1:8 *106, 110*
2 *106*
8 *106*
10 *106*
13–28 *106*

Romans

1 *145*
1:24 *146*
1:26 *146*
1:28 *146*
5:8 *35*
8:1 *28, 59, 143, 157*
8:9 *82*
8:18 *65, 195*
8:25 *195*
8:31–39 *28*
12:14 *157*
12:14–21 *148*
12:17–20 *157*

1 Corinthians

3:10–15 *154*
3:16 *76*
3:16–17 *169, 172*
5:7 *128*
6:18–20 *80*
6:19 *76, 172*
6:19–20 *44*
13:12 *173*
15:20 *132*
15:26 *32, 113, 155, 186*
15:51–57 *113*

219

2 Corinthians
1:21–22 *76*
1:22 *18, 28, 59*
5:5 *60*
5:10 *154*
6:16 *161, 169, 172*
11:2 *168*
12:9–10 *109*
13:1 *109*

Galatians
3:6–8 *64*
5:19–24 *77*
6:7 *147*

Ephesians
1:13 *18, 28, 59*
1:13–14 *76*
1:14 *60, 117*
2:21–22 *169, 172*
2:22 *76*
4 *81*
4:15 *148*
4:30 *28, 59*
5:25–33 *168*
5:27 *117*
6 *184*
6:10–20 *85*
6:12 *90*
6:13 *184*

Philippians
1:6 *60*
1:19 *82*
2:15 *117*

Colossians
1:18 *131*
1:22–23 *117*

1 Timothy
5:19 *109*
6:16 *41*

2 Timothy
2:19 *77*
3:12 *89, 182*

Hebrews
3:6 *172*
9:14 *117*
10:31 *157*
12:1–2 *119*
12:2 *192*

James
4:7 *92*

1 Peter
1:11 *82*
1:18–19 *44*
1:19 *117*
2:4–5 *172*
2:5 *169*
5:9 *92*
5:13 *13, 33*

2 Peter
2:9 *113*
3:8–9 *34*
3:9 *153*

1 John
1:5 *41*
2:18 *94*
3:16 *127*
4:4 *60*
4:19 *107, 191*

Jude
24 *117*

Revelation
1 *35, 54, 128*
1:1 *4, 8, 121, 136, 137*
1:1–2 *4*

224

18:5–7 *146*
18:8 *90*
18:9–19 *148*
18:10 *13*
18:11–16 *105*
18–19 *148*
18:20 *34, 47, 114, 149*
18:20–19:5 *148*
18:21 *13*
18:23 *16, 105*
18:23–24 *149*
18:24 *5, 57, 111, 181*
19 *39, 45, 50, 95, 134, 137, 149, 153*
19:1–2 *34*
19:1–3 *167*
19:1–4 *47*
19:1–5 *49*
19:1–8 *50, 170*
19:2 *5, 15, 57, 114, 149, 181*
19:6–7 *45, 163*
19:6–8 *49, 167*
19:6–10 *19, 134*
19:6–20:15 *134*
19:7 *45, 127, 162, 168*
19:7–8 *14, 116, 162, 168, 191*
19:8 *168*
19:9 *98, 127, 163, 175, 195*
19:10 *8, 48, 56, 73, 83, 191*
19:11 *108*
19:11–16 *96, 135, 137*
19:11–21 *134, 153, 162*
19:14 *100, 154*
19:15 *108, 123, 150*
19:16 *133*
19:17–18 *15*
19:17–21 *135*
19:19 *100*
19:19–21 *94, 96, 158*
19:20 *14, 16, 28, 135, 153, 155*

19:21 *108*
19–22 *15*
20 *33, 97, 101, 153, 154, 158*
20:1 *13*
20:2 *17, 27*
20:2–3 *162*
20:3 *13*
20:4 *16, 56, 58, 77, 111, 120, 149, 162, 191*
20:4–6 *154, 162, 163, 171, 181*
20:6 *98, 149, 162, 195*
20:7–8 *153*
20:7–10 *91, 162*
20:7–15 *153, 158*
20:8 *16, 104*
20:8–10 *167*
20:9 *154*
20:10 *14, 154, 155*
20:11 *143*
20:11–15 *15, 97, 143, 154*
20:12 *154*
20:13 *14*
20:14 *14, 33, 132, 155, 162*
20:14–15 *14*
20:15 *154, 155, 163*
21 *28, 39, 67, 97, 169*
21:1 *160, 162, 164*
21:1–7 *64, 67, 177*
21:1–8 *17, 175*
21:2 *45, 160, 162, 164, 169, 175*
21:3 *31, 79, 162, 163, 173*
21:3–5 *166*
21:4 *28, 132, 155, 162, 163, 166, 173*
21:4–5 *166*
21:5 *44, 163, 164, 173*
21:5–6 *23*
21:6 *23, 81, 123, 162, 163, 166*
21:6–7 *97*

225

226